KEITH RICHARDS
ON KEITH RICHARDS
INTERVIEWS & ENCOUNTERS

OTHER BOOKS IN THE *MUSICIANS IN THEIR OWN WORDS* SERIES

Springsteen on Springsteen: Interviews, Speeches and Encounters

KEITH RICHARDS
ON KEITH RICHARDS
INTERVIEWS & ENCOUNTERS

EDITED BY SEAN EGAN

OMNIBUS PRESS
London / New York / Paris / Sydney / Copenhagen / Berlin / Madrid / Tokyo

Copyright © 2013 Sean Egan
This edition published in 2014 by Omnibus Press
(A Division of Music Sales Limited)

This edition published by arrangement with Chicago Review Press.

ISBN: 978.1.783.05356.8
Order No: OP55605

Interior design: Jonathan Hahn
Cover photograph: Paul Natkin/Getty Images

Exclusive Distributors
Music Sales Limited,
14/15 Berners Street,
London, W1T 3LJ.

Macmillan Distribution Services,
56 Parkwest Drive
Derrimut, Vic 3030,
Australia.

Every effort has been made to trace the copyright holders of the photographs in
this book but one or two were unreachable. We would be grateful if the photogra-
phers concerned would contact us.

Printed in the EU.

A catalogue record for this book is available from the British Library.

Visit Omnibus Press on the web at www.omnibuspress.com

CONTENTS

INTRODUCTION

Whether it be "The Human Riff," "Mr. Rock 'n' Roll," "Keith Riff-hard," "The World's Most Elegantly Wasted Human Being," or just "Keef," his nicknames speak volumes about the affection held by the rock fraternity for the man who has been the joint most important member of the Rolling Stones for half a century.

In the Stones' early years, Keith Richards—born December 18, 1943— was professionally known as "Keith Richard" and was unquestionably to the rear of both Stones singer Mick Jagger and fellow guitarist Brian Jones in terms of importance, renown, and prominence. The vocalist was naturally the focal point for both media and fans. Jones not only vied with Jagger for status of fan favorite courtesy of his golden good looks but was in demand from journalists impressed by his eloquence and gravitas-conveying posh tones. Nonetheless, that fan favorite principle—the notion that each member of a pop group possessed his own devotees— meant that Richards's views always received at least a by-rotation exposure in the music press.

Richards's position equidistant between the glamour of Jagger and Jones and the semi-anonymity of "Quiet Ones" Charlie Watts (drums) and Bill Wyman (bass) began to shift in 1965 with the release of the Stones' first self-generated UK single, "The Last Time." Courtesy of the phenomenally successful songwriting partnership he developed with Jagger, Richards was transformed within months from merely one of hundreds of Western musicians purveying versions of other people's songs to half of the second-most important songwriting partnership in the world. That Stones fare like "(I Can't Get No) Satisfaction," "Get Off of My Cloud," and "Let's Spend the Night Together" was not just aesthetically brilliant but the exquisite articulation of the grievances of a fractious young generation made Richards and his opinions sociologically significant. In 1967, Richards acquired a fame beyond the parameters of the pop business when a drug bust at his house Redlands and—in the company of Jagger—subsequent trial and brief imprisonment catapulted him onto the front pages of British national newspapers.

Journalists increasingly began requesting quotes from the guitarist, genuinely keen to get his perspective rather than grumpily settling for it in lieu of Jagger's or Jones's availability. Richards blossomed with his increasing importance, the taciturn, big-eared, acne-scarred ruffian of the early days transformed into a stylish physical symbol of the rebellious spirit of rock music. It wasn't all image either. Kicking an audience member in the face for spitting, punching a journalist in the jaw for suggesting the July 1969 Hyde Park concert was disrespectful to the memory of the just-deceased Jones, and squaring up to Hell's Angels at the December 1969 Altamont festival suggested a man who walked it like he talked it. For all these reasons, by the early 1970s, wannabe rock stars and regional rebels across the world were imitating Richards's big belt buckles, trailing scarves, shark tooth necklace, mirrored shades, and—especially—tangled, shoulder-length mane of black hair.

When Richards made the front cover of *Rolling Stone* in August 1971, it served to confirm that he was now a counter-cultural icon as important as Jagger. As the 1970s wore on, he became more than even that. Jagger's hitherto unassailable position as scourge of the authoritarian establishment whose fusty values his generation sought to overthrow began to look increasingly suspect as he hobnobbed with the type of dignitaries and socialites with whom Richards wouldn't be seen dead. Meanwhile, thrillingly for some, Richards being seen dead became an increasingly likely prospect: knowledge of his heroin addiction was an open secret much discussed in the music papers, as well as in the mainstream press on the occasions of his frequent arrests. The outlaw image engendered by Richards's implicit defiance of the authorities and his tangoing with the Grim Reaper communicated to the rock audience a retention of anti-establishment integrity. Though that logic might have been confused, he at least provided a dramatic counterpoint in his druggie murk to Jagger's glitzy carryings-on. Richards's infamous 1977 Toronto drug bust ended that "wasted" lifestyle where the responsibility of raising two children and the trauma of the death of a third had not. Although the prospect of a life sentence for trafficking brought about his cleanup, Richards dines out on his smack decade to this day. It gave him a myth that Stones fans and journalists are more than happy to indulge and bolster. Richards, in turn, cooperates in the process by turning horror stories of addled irresponsibility into funny anecdotes. He may now be more or less law-abiding, but his outlaw aura will never die.

On one level, Richards's interviews have been what one would expect of a man with his image. His spurning of banality and rejection of euphemism were right in line with that no-nonsense rebel mien. Yet, other aspects of his character revealed by his increasingly frequent audiences with the press were surprising. Few journalists came away from a Richards interview without noting in print how warm and unpretentious was a man who one might more readily assume to be aloof, sinister, and self-regarding. Moreover, he was an unusually articulate and intelligent individual. Witness how the aforesaid 1971 *Rolling Stone* interview is speckled with comments that reveal a man steeped in the hardly rock 'n' roll subject of history. He was also perennially honest, answering questions about sensitive subjects like band interrelations, the death of Brian Jones, and personal drug use with a degree of candor Jagger was too haughty (some would say sensible) to even entertain.

Richards is not always a reliable witness. Checking his versions of events against the known facts reveals that he tends to conflate or telescope incidents for reasons of poetry. This leads to such widely disseminated myths as the story of Stones manager Andrew Loog Oldham locking him and Jagger in a kitchen and not letting them out until they'd written their first song. Though the incident is not a complete fabrication, Jagger and Oldham's separate testimonies suggest that the reality was more mundane and elongated than Richards's recollection would have it. Moreover, as he has gotten older, the Richards persona has become encrusted with a submission to tabloid cliché. From the early 1980s onward, he began playing up to his image of rock outlaw via stylized self-deprecation about his days as a bad boy and menace to society, something that has become embarrassingly pronounced in recent years, although no less so than his verbal usage of Americanisms like "baby." However, his frankness continues to outweigh his posturing. This became an ever more important asset as the decades wore on: whereas Mick Jagger's interviews have become exercises in obfuscation and almost irritatingly sustained politesse, Richards's have remained likeable, open, and scathing about cant.

This collection spans the five decades of the Rolling Stones' career. It contains Richards interviews from such celebrated publications as *Melody Maker*, *Rolling Stone*, *Zigzag*, *Record Collector*, and *GQ* as well as interviews that have never previously appeared in print. It charts the journey of Richards from gauche young pretender to swaggering epitome of the zeitgeist to beloved elder statesman of rock. Some may find the values of the Richards of yore objectionable. Some may be dismayed by the pantomime persona Richards has latterly become. Few would dispute, however, that these pages illustrate that when Keith Richards sits down in front of a microphone, a certain kind of magic occurs.

—Sean Egan

1 |

I'D LIKE TO FORGET ABOUT *JUKE BOX JURY* SAYS KEITH RICHARD

KEITH RICHARDS | 1964

This ghostwritten Richards column from Britain's now-defunct music weekly *Melody Maker* is an interesting snapshot of the Stones in mid-July 1964, a year and one month after the release of their debut single. The guitarist uses his turn in the spotlight to praise some fellow "beat" groups, bang the drum for R&B, and comment on the Stones' first number one in any of the four competing British charts. The bulk of the column, though, is understandably dedicated to a very controversial appearance the Stones had made a week before on record review TV show *Juke Box Jury*, where they had the temerity to be sniffy about almost every new release they were played, including the latest by the exalted Elvis Presley. Richards—as straight-talking then as he is now—shrugs his shoulders at the furor. Such exhibitions of sullen indifference to public opinion were then uncommon and only bolstered the group's burgeoning image as champions of the younger generation's rebellious ideals.

All right, so Juke Box Jury wasn't a knockout. Now everybody's had a go at us, I'd like the chance to reply.

I think the whole programme's very limited for a start. We all sat, consciously, knowing there were five of us, and we had a few seconds each after each record.

We weren't great, and that's a fact. But the records they played us! They were NOTHING! Don't misunderstand— they weren't bad records, but there didn't seem anything to say about them.

It wasn't that the singing or guitars were out of tune on any particular record, but they were all records with nothing much about them. We were lost. And I think it came across.

We were all lost, except for Charlie and maybe Mick. I agree we didn't come over well, but it wouldn't be much different if we did it again, quite honestly.

It's the way the show's run that restricts you. Juke Box Jury doesn't suit the Stones.

I'll say one thing for our show on Juke Box, though. I'm sure that's what helped us reach number one. If nothing else, it kept our image up!

People thought the worst of us before they saw us. When they finally looked at Juke Box Jury, it was the confirmation that we were a bunch of idiots.

We don't care that much what people think. But I can tell you this: it's difficult to say anything sensible in a few seconds, especially with unspectacular records. But I could tell things were not going well on the show.

We don't particularly care about whether we go back on the Jury. It was an experience I personally would rather forget.

Having a number one hit's a good feeling, but we're not all mad about it.

I'd hate everybody to think that just because we've made the top spot this time, we'll have to do it every time we have a single out. All the Stones agree that as long as we get in the top ten, we'll be very happy.

As it happens, I think "It's All Over Now" is the best single we've done, and I'm glad to say the group improves every time it makes a single. At least, we think so.

I like the overall sound on this new one more than I did on anything before.

Glad Mick wrote a bit last week about the Paramounts. We all think they're good and deserve to make it.

Wayne Fontana has a very good group, though. Give them the right material and they'll be there.

It's all very well people having a go at the rhythm-and-blues thing and saying it's not authentic.

But there's a lot more good come out of the scene than many people allow.

For instance, the trad boom didn't do much good for the real thing, did it? People only got interested in British copies of the real thing.

Now, in R&B, people are digging British groups—and if you look at the chart you get big names like Howlin' Wolf, Chuck Berry, Bo Diddley and Tommy Tucker.

That's what's really pleased me about it all. If our stuff has got people interested in R&B by some of the great American stars, we'll have done some good.

I personally reckon that this can be built up. The next step for groups like ours could be to do more gospel. Pop music tastes are changing, and I don't see why we can't get people interested in such people as Solomon Burke.

I don't think he's selling very big, but I'd like him to, because he's great.

People who knock the R&B scene don't give it enough credit for interesting people in something they'd never have heard of.

I'm fed up of people calling us non-authentic. Why can't we play what we like?

Who's laying down the rules?

2 |

KEITH TALKS ABOUT SONGWRITING

KEITH RICHARDS | 1964

The Rolling Stones Book was a monthly from Beat Publications released to cash in on the success of the group in the same way that the same stable's *The Beatles Book* had already capitalized on the ascendency of the Fab Four. During its lifetime from June 1964 to November 1966, the fact that *The Rolling Stones Book* had three dozen or so pages to fill on a regular basis with purely Stones material meant that every member received exposure. Though the boast that the "boys" edited it themselves can be taken with a pinch of salt, the monthly often saw the band speaking more frankly and indeed caustically than they did in the music press (although to be fair, the music press in those days would probably have toned down any controversial remarks on the grounds that they might upset their readers).

This feature from the third issue of the magazine, dated August 10, 1964, captures Richards at a point where he, with Jagger, was just dipping his toes into the forbidding pool that was songwriting.

Note: for "Marion Faithful" read "Marianne Faithfull."

Mick and I have been writing songs together for about a year now. We didn't make a lot of fuss about it when we started, we just began working at it, because it was something that we both like doing.

In fact, very few people realised that we did write songs until Gene Pitney recorded "That Girl Belongs to Yesterday." Gene's a big mate of ours and has helped us terrifically by turning that particular number into a big hit.

You never know how things are going to turn out in this business, but being a professional songwriter would suit me fine.

Two other numbers of ours are out now. "As Tears Go By" has been recorded by the new girl singer, Marion Faithful, and our version of "Tell Me" has been released as a single in the States, and I understand it's doing very well over there.

At the moment, we've got about a dozen songs sort of half finished. Most of them are intended for our next L.P. but we've got a lot of work to do on them yet and it gets more and more difficult to find time every week. Sometimes, we can finish a song in ten minutes, but others hang around for months on end.

I usually write the music with a title in mind, then Mick adds the words. I can't write a note of music, of course, but then neither could most of the best songwriters of the last fifty years. I don't find any difficulty as I've got a very good memory and can easily complete a song after I've been keeping the bits in my head for several weeks.

If I suddenly get what I think is a good idea, I do sometimes put it on tape but not very often. Mick's just the same—how he remembers words which he first thought of a month or so back, I just don't know.

Every songwriter has a number of songs which he wished he'd written. All of Dionne Warwick's stuff—in fact, anything by Burt Bacharach and Hal David. Those two are really brilliant. Their ideas are so original.

The great thing about songwriting is that despite the thousands and thousands of songs which have been written there are still so many melodies yet to be discovered. But, one thing I still have not been able to do— that's write a number good enough for the Stones to use as an "A" side in England. Most of the numbers that Mick and I write are pretty complicated whilst the Stones need relatively simple ones with very few chord changes in them. But, it does sound crazy saying that we can't write stuff for the Stones when we're part of them.

Of course, my big ambition is to have lots of hits but, also, I would like to have our songs recorded by lots of different artistes. I'd love to see what someone like Dionne Warwick would do with some of our numbers. No, that's daft, ANYTHING she did with them would please me. I like the music business so much that if I didn't make it with song writing I think

I'd have a bash at being a record producer aiming at selling my discs in both the British and American markets. Trouble in this country is that practically every British artiste is established in his or her own style and it gets more and more difficult to create anything new. In the States, on the other hand, they are forever experimenting and getting new sounds. Often nowadays, the Americans only put a rhythm section on records but it comes out sounding like a full orchestra. It's fantastic!

Being a record producer is a tough job but I think I could handle it. Andrew Oldham takes our sessions now, but all of the Stones have a say in what goes on and it's terrific experience. Really I wouldn't like to do the whole job on my own, I'd rather have someone working with me, like Mick for example. I don't think that any one person can possibly get all the ideas.

In my opinion, many record producers are in a rut. There are so many new sounds floating around just waiting to be discovered, and only people like Phil Spector and Andrew Oldham, are brave enough to experiment with them. I'd like to try and get a variation on the American group sound, with the singers sounding like part of the orchestration. The 4 Seasons, who are very big in the States, are one of the best examples of this.

I don't think that there's any other form of recording I'd like to tackle, simply because you can't express yourself if you have to keep to a style that has been fixed already. Apart from songwriting and record-producing, the only other ambition I've got is to buy a huge house on a small tropical island where it's always about 100°. I'd just sit in the sun all day and have some servants (including Mick Jagger) looking after me! That would be my idea of heaven!

3 |

SUE MAUTNER TAKES YOU ROUND KEITH'S HOUSE

SUE MAUTNER | 1966

Keith Richards's picturesque thatched, moated West Sussex house Redlands looms large in his legend, not least because it was the location of a drug bust in 1967; the trial that resulted underlined the Stones' anti-establishment credentials. A series of mysterious fires at the property that generated nudge-nudge, wink-wink public discussion of their causes is another reason for Redlands's high-profile. Though published only the year before the famous bust, Sue Mautner's article for issue 25 of *The Rolling Stones Book* captures Richards's occupation of Redlands at a far more innocent and carefree time.

A couple of the staff mentioned in passing also play a part in Richards's legend. The chauffer—Patrick—is the man Richards has long suspected tipped off the police about the Redlands drug party they raided. The gardener may well be horticulturist-with-a-large-tread Jack Dyer, inspiration for "Jumpin' Jack Flash."

Fortunately it was a beautiful sunny day when I drove down to Keith's fifteenth century house in Sussex, because "Mr Richard hasn't arrived yet," said the old gardener as I approached the drive.

Fortunate for me because after driving for two-and-a-half hours I had become somewhat stuck to the seat of my car, so it was a good opportunity to stretch my legs and generally nose around the beautiful thatched-roofed house, which is surrounded by a moat on which float some very talkative ducks—obviously they were talking about the weather, what else!

I walked round the back of the house to find a horse grazing in the next field, which later on I found out belonged to Keith—not the horse but the field (he just happened to loan the field to its owner). Lying on the beautifully mowed lawn was a rather old-looking paddle boat—obviously that would also be explained later. As I wandered towards the back of the house there was a dartboard hanging up on the stone wall, and I guessed that someone had been there before—quite a clever piece of detection, because the darts had been left in. Much to my surprise (and only because I was being so nosy) I found the porch door open, so I took the liberty of entering.

The first room I found myself in was the lounge—no furniture, just a massive oak-panelled room with parquet flooring, wooden beams, two enormous stone pillars and a huge stone fireplace with a gigantic flute coming down the chimney. Keith had already moved some of his belongings because there was a white fur rug on the floor, an electric piano, a harpsichord and a guitar plus his record and book collection and of course his hi-fi.

I was very interested and surprised to learn that his books consisted of "The Great War," "Dictionary of Slang," "Guns," "Great Sea Battles," "Drawings of Rembrandt" and books on England, and even more surprised with his record collection. Amongst the Beatles, Otis Redding, Dylan, Simon and Garfunkel, the Everlys, the Temptations and Elvis were albums of "Chopin's Nineteen Waltzes," Rossini and Segovia.

Half an hour had gone by and still no sign of Keith, so I picked up the phone and dialled his office. "Sorry Sue, tried to get you before but you'd left. Keith's been held up at a meeting but he shouldn't be very long," came the reply. So I decided the best thing to do was to look over the rest of the house. But before I ventured upstairs I placed a record on the player.

The upstairs consisted of five bedrooms and a bathroom, I knew which was Keith's room, because the bed was unmade, and there was a pair of shoes and a Dennis Wheatley book lying on the floor. All the rooms were unfurnished and like the downstairs it was all wooden beams and floors. One bedroom had half the floor missing so I could see immediately into the kitchen.

One side of an L.P. later I came downstairs through the large dining room and into the kitchen to find some dirty dishes, a burnt sausage in the frying pan on the cooker, a rifle on the wall, a spur hanging on the other wall and a clock on the door, not to mention a truncheon hanging from the ceiling (Keith pinched it off of a gendarme in Paris). Being a female my immediate reaction was to put the kettle on for a cuppa. Whilst selecting my next record the kettle began to whistle furiously, I remembered spotting a bottle of milk in the passage between the garage and the house, so I left the kettle whistling and went out to fetch the milk which a stray cat had got to before me, nevertheless he wasn't clever enough to open it.

As I was pouring out my tea Keith drove up in his Bentley Continental plus L plates and Patrick.

"Sorry I'm late, how did you get in?" Keith was very annoyed with the builders for leaving the house unlocked, so it was just as well I arrived early.

"Hope you don't mind me making myself at home," I said, "have a cup of tea."

"What do you think of the place?", said Keith, "of course it's not furnished yet, I want to do it bit by bit. I'm going to mix the furniture and have modern and Tudor.

"As you can see," said Keith pointing to some old chests, "I've bought some pieces off of the people who lived here before. I'm going to have mauve paint in the dining room and probably the lounge and spotlights on the walls. I've got this interior decorator who did the *Queen Mary* as it is today.

"Come and take a look outside. I'm having a wall built round the front of the house, which will now be the back if you see what I mean, because I'm extending the path round to the back and making it the front. Anyway I think this should be the front because it's got a porch, and the only reason you think the other side is the front, is because of the drive."

"Who's boat is that?" I enquired. "Oh, that belonged to the owner, I bought it off him, you can paddle round the moat in it, but at the moment it's got a hole in the side!"

"See that cottage over there," said Keith pointing to just outside the grounds. "As it's so cheap I'm going to buy it and have a couple of staff living there. A husband and wife preferably, so she can cook and clean the house, and he can do all the odd jobs. At the moment the gardener comes in everyday except Thursday."

As we went back inside I mentioned to Keith that whilst nosing around I noticed some sound-proof equipment in the garage. "Yes, I'm turning one of the bedrooms into a recording studio. There's so much to be done, I'm knocking down walls and blocking out doors. Downstairs I'm making a small cloakroom for people to hang their coats in, and wait till you see the kitchen finished, I've got this cooker which disappears into the wall.

"You know, it's marvellously situated here. There's a little shopping village where you just ring up and they send your order round, and also I'm only a mile from the sea."

Patrick poked his head round the door to tell Keith that his bacon and eggs were ready. Keith put on a Simon and Garfunkel album and we joined him in the kitchen.

"I'm still going to keep my London flat, because if I've been to a party or something it will be too late to drive all the way down here. I'm also going to get a run-around car, something like a Mustang or even a jeep."

Keith polished-off his bacon and eggs and said he had to be off, as he was catching a plane to Cannes. "I'm going there just for a couple of days," said Keith putting on his fur jacket which one would expect a woman to wear.

"Do you like it, I bought it off this girl for £20 'cos she was broke," said Keith as he stepped into his Bentley plus his L plates!

4 |

THE *ROLLING STONE* INTERVIEW: KEITH RICHARD

ROBERT GREENFIELD | 1971

Robert Greenfield's epic, rambling interview with Richards in the August 19, 1971, issue of *Rolling Stone* was significant on two counts. First, courtesy of the amazingly candid answers of its subject, it provided a permanent treasure trove of research material for Stones scholars. The second was that it served to thrust Richards center stage in the public consciousness with Mick Jagger. Although the show business convention that had led to the Stones' lead singer being granted the most attention had been eroded over recent years, Richards's being featured on the ultra-cool magazine's cover and across twelve of its oversize interior pages confirmed once and for all that the guitarist was no mere sidekick. He was now well on his way to the status of living embodiment of rock 'n' roll.

Most reprints of this interview—even those published by *Rolling Stone*—omit large chunks. This is a rare unexpurgated publication.

Note: for "Marlan" read "Marlon."

for "Alan Klein" read "Allen Klein."

Keith plays in a rock & roll band. Anita is a movie star queen. They currently reside in a large white marble house that everyone describes as "decadent looking." The British Admiral who built it had trees brought from all over the world in ships of the line, pine and cypress and palm. There is an exotic colored bird in a cage in the front garden and a rabbit called Boots that lives in the back. A dog named Oakie sleeps where he wants.

Meals are the only recurring reality and twenty three at a table is not an unusual number. The ceilings are thirty feet from the floor and some nights, pink lightning hangs over the bay and the nearby town of Ville-france, which waits for the fleet to come back so its hotels can turn again into whorehouses.

There is a private beach down a flight of stairs and a water bed on the porch. Good reference points for the whole mise-en-scène are F. Scott Fitzgerald's "Tender Is the Night" and the Shirelles' greatest hits. There is a piano in the living room and guitars in the TV room. Between George Jones, Merle Haggard, Buddy Holly, and Chuck Berry, Keith Richard manages to sneak in a lick now and then like a great acoustic version of "The Jerk" by the Larks one morning at 4 AM.

A recording studio will soon be completed in the basement and the Stones will go to work on some tracks for the new album, Mick Jagger having returned from his honeymoon. They will tour the States soon.

Most of it is in the tapes, in the background. Two cogent statements, both made by Keith may be kept in mind while reading the questions and answers (which were asked and answered over a ten-day period at odd hours).

"It's a pretty good house; we're doing our best to fill it up with kids and rock 'n' roll."

"You know that thing that Blind Willie said? 'I don't like the suits and ties / They don't seem to harmonize.'"

What were you doing right at the beginning?
I was hanging out at art school. Yeah. Suburban art school. I mean in England, if you're lucky you get into art school. It's somewhere they put you if they can't put you anywhere else. If you can't saw wood straight or file metal. It's where they put me to learn graphic design because I happened to be good at drawing apples or something. Fifteen . . . I was there for three years and meanwhile I learned how to play guitar. Lotta guitar players in art school. A lot of terrible artists too. It's funny.

Your parents weren't musical?
Nah. My grandfather was. He used to have a dance band in the Thirties. Played the sax. Was in a country band in the late Fifties, too, playin' the US bases in England. Gus Dupree . . . King of the Country Fiddle. He was

a groove, y'know . . . a good musician . . . He was never professional for more than a few years in the Thirties.

What did your father do?
He had a variety of professions. He was a baker for a while. I know he got shot up in the First World War. Gassed or something.

Were you raised middle class?
Working class. English working class . . . struggling, thinking they were middle class. Moved into a tough neighborhood when I was about ten. I used to be with Mick before that . . . we used to live close together. Then I moved to what they'd call in the States a housing project. Just been built. Thousands and thousands of houses, everyone wondering what the fuck was going on. Everyone was displaced. They were still building it and really there were gangs everywhere. Coming to Teddy Boys. Just before rock and roll hit England. But they were all waiting for it. They were practicing.

Were you one of the boys?
Rock and roll got me into being one of the boys. Before that I just got me ass kicked all over the place. Learned how to ride a punch.

It's strange, 'cause I knew Mick when I was really young . . . five, six, seven. We used to hang out together. Then I moved and didn't see him for a long time. I once met him selling ice creams outside the public library. I bought one. He was tryin' to make extra money.

Rock and roll got to England about '53, '54, you were eleven . . .
Yeah. Presley hit first. Actually, the music from Blackboard Jungle, "Rock Around the Clock," hit first. Not the movie, just the music. People saying, "Ah, did ya hear that music, man." Because in England, we had never heard anything. It's still the same scene: BBC controls it.

Then, everybody stood up for that music. I didn't think of playing it. I just wanted to go and listen to it. It took 'em a year or so before anyone in England could make that music. The first big things that hit were skiffle— simple three chord stuff. It wasn't really rock and roll. It was a lot more folky, a lot more strummy. Tea chest basses. A very crude sort of rock and roll. Lonnie Donegan's the only cat to come out of skiffle.

But we were really listening to what was coming from over the Atlantic. The ones that were hitting hard were Little Richard and Presley and Jerry Lee Lewis. Chuck Berry was never really that big in England. They dug him but . . . all his big big hits made it . . . but maybe because he never came over. Maybe because the movies he made like *Go Johnny Go* never got over because of distribution problems. Fats Domino was big. Freddie Bell and the Bellboys too; all kinds of weird people that never made it in America.

They loved the piano. Looking back on it, all the piano boys really had it together for England. More than just the cat that stood there with the guitar.

Did you start really playing in school then?
Yeah. It's funny going back that far. Things come through but . . . I'll tell you who's really good at pushing memories: Bill. He's got this little mind that remembers everything. I'm sure it's like he rolls a tape.

How things were at the start is something. It's when everybody's got short hair. And everybody thought it was long. That's the thing. I mean, we were really being put down like shit then for having long hair. Really. Now, people go into offices with longer hair.

When I went to art school, people were just startin' to grow their hair and loosen up. You got in there on the favors of the headmaster. You go there and show him your shit, the stuff you've done at ordinary school, during art lessons, and he decides. You don't have to do anything apart from going to see him. He says, "You takin' anything? What are you on?" And you're about 15 or 16 and you don't even know what the fuck they do in art school. You have this vague picture of naked ladies sittin' around. Drawing them . . . well, I'll try that.

So you go there and you get your packet of Five Weights [cigarettes] a day. Everybody's broke . . . and the best thing that's going on is in the bog [toilet] with the guitars. There's always some cat sneaked out going through his latest Woody Guthrie tune or Jack Elliot. Everybody's into that kind of music as well. So when I went to art school I was thrown into that end of it too. Before that I was just into Little Richard. I was rockin' away, avoidin' the bicycle chains and the razors in those dance halls. The English get crazy. They're calm, but they were really violent then, those cats. Those suits cost them $150, which is a lot of money. Jackets down to here. Waistcoats. Leopardskin lapels . . . amazing. It was really "Don't step on mah blue suede shoes." It was down to that.

I really, literally, got myself thrown out of school. I was livin' at home but I had to go everyday. When you think that kids, all they really want to do is learn, watch how it's done and try and figure out why and leave it at that. You're going to school to do something you wanna do and they manage to turn the whole thing around and make you hate 'em. They really manage to do it. I don't know anyone at that school who liked it or anyone my age who liked to be at school. One or two people who went to a decent school had a good teacher, someone who really knew how to teach. The nearest thing I been to it is Wormwood Scrubbs [an English prison] and that's the nick. Really, it's the same feeling.

So you spent three years there and it was coming to degree time . . .
That's when they got me. It was 1958, they chucked me out. It's amazing—Lennon, all those people, were already playing. I hadn't really thought about playing. I was still just jivin' to it. I went straight into this art school, and I heard these cats playing', heard they were layin' down some Broonzy songs. And I suddenly realized it goes back a lot further than just the two years I'd been listenin'. And I picked up the nearest guitar and started learnin' from these cats. I learned from all these amateur art school people. One cat knew how to play "Cocaine Blues" very well, another cat knew how to play something else very well. There were a lot better guitar players at school than me.

But then I started to get into where it had come from. Broonzy first. He and Josh White were considered to be the only living black bluesmen still playing. So let's get that together, I thought, that can't be right. Then I started to discover Robert Johnson and those cats. You could never get their records though. One heard about them. On one hand I was playing all that folk stuff on the guitar. The other half of me was listenin' to all that rock and roll, Chuck Berry, and sayin' yeah, yeah.

And one day, I met Jagger again, man. Of all places, on the fucking train. I was going to the school and he was going up to the London School of Economics. It was about 1960. I never been able to get this one together, it's so strange. I had these two things going and not being able to plug 'em together, playing guitar like all the other cats, folk, a little blues. But you can't get the sounds from the States. Maybe once every six months someone'll come through with an album, an Arhoolie album of Fred McDowell. And you'd say: There's another cat! That's another one. Just blowin' my mind, like one album every six months.

So I get on this train one morning and there's Jagger and under his arm he has four or five albums. I haven't seen him since the time I bought an ice cream off him and we haven't hung around since we were five, six, ten years. We recognized each other straight off. "Hi, man," I say. "Where ya going?" he says. And under his arm, he's got Chuck Berry and Little Walter, Muddy Waters. "You're into Chuck Berry, man, really?" That's a coincidence. He said, "Yeah, I got few more albums. Been writin' away to this, uh, Chess Records in Chicago and got a mailing list thing and . . . got it together, you know?" Wow, man!

So I invited him up to my place for a cup of tea. He started playing me these records and I really turned on to it. We were both still living in Dartford, on the edge of London and I was still in art school.

There was another cat at art school named Dick Taylor, who later got the Pretty Things together. Mick found out—"Oh, you play?" he said to me. That's what amazed him. Mick had been singin' with some rock and roll bands, doin' Buddy Holly. . . Buddy Holly was in England as solid as Elvis. Everything came out was a record smash number one. By about '58, it was either Elvis or Buddy Holly. It was split into two camps. The Elvis fans were the heavy leather boys and the Buddy Holly ones all somehow looked like Buddy Holly.

By that time, the initial wham had gone out of rock and roll. You were getting "By the Light of the Silvery Moon" by Little Richard and "My Blue Heaven" by Fats, "Baby Face." They'd run out of songs in a way, it seemed like. England itself was turning on to its own breed of rock and rollers. Cliff Richard at the time was a big rocker. Adam Faith. Billy Fury, who did one fantastic album that I've lost. He got it together once. One really good album. Songs he'd written, like people do now, he got some people he knew to play together and did it. His other scene was the hits, heavy moody ballads and the lead pipe down the trousers. They were all into that one.

To get back to Mick and I . . . He found out that I could play a little and he could sing a bit. "I dig to sing," he said, and he also knew Dick Taylor from another school they'd gone to and the thing tied up so we try and do something. We'd all go to Dick Taylor's house, in his back room, some other cats would come along and play, and we'd try to lay some of this Little Walter stuff and Chuck Berry stuff. No drummer or anything. Just two guitars and a little amplifier. Usual back room stuff. It fell into place very quickly.

Then we found Slim Harpo, we started to really find people. Mick was just singing, no harp. And suddenly in '62, just when we were getting together, we read this little thing about a rhythm and blues club starting in Ealing. Everybody must have been trying to get one together. "Let's go up to this place and find out what's happening." There was this amazing old cat playing harp . . . Cyril Davies. Where did he come from? He turned out to be a panel beater from North London. He was a great cat, Cyril. He didn't last long. I only knew him for about two years and he died.

Alexis Korner really got this scene together. He'd been playin' in jazz clubs for ages and he knew all the connections for gigs. So we went up there. The first or the second time Mick and I were sittin' there Alexis Korner gets up and says, "We got a guest to play some guitar. He comes from Cheltenham. All the way up from Cheltenham just to play for ya."

Suddenly, it's *Elmore James*, this cat, man. And it's *Brian*, man, he sittin' on his little . . . he's bent over . . . da-da-da, da-da-da . . . I said, what? What the fuck? Playing bar slide guitar.

We get into Brian after he finishes "Dust My Blues." He's really fantastic and a gas. We speak to Brian. He'd been doin' the same as we'd been doin' . . . thinkin' he was the only cat in the world who was doin' it. We started to turn Brian on to some Jimmy Reed things, Chicago blues that he hadn't heard. He was more into T-Bone Walker and jazz-blues stuff. We'd turn him on to Chuck Berry and say, "Look, it's all the same shit, man, and you can do it." But Brian was also much more together. He was in the process of getting a band together and moving up to London with one of his many women and children. God knows how many he had. He sure left his mark, that cat. I know of five kids, at least. All by different chicks, and they all look like Brian.

He was a good guitar player then. He had the touch and was just peaking. He was already out of school, he'd been kicked out of university and had a variety of jobs. He was already into living on his own and trying to find a pad for his old lady. Whereas Mick and I were just kicking around in back rooms, still living at home.

I left art school and I didn't even bother to get a job. We were still kids. Mick was still serious, he thought he was, everyone told him he ought to be serious about a career in economics. He was very much into it.

But Brian, he was already working at it. We said, "We're just amateurs, man, but we dig to play." He invited me up to listen to what he was getting together in some pub in London. It's then it starts getting into back rooms of pubs in Soho and places. That's where I met Stew [Ian Stewart]. He was with Brian. They'd just met. He used to play boogie-woogie piano in jazz clubs, apart from his regular job. He blew my head off too, when he started to play. I never heard a white piano like that before. Real Albert Ammons stuff. This is all '62.

A lot of these old cats had been playin' blues in those clubs for ages, or thought they were playin' blues. Just because they'd met Big Bill Broonzy at a party or played with him once, they thought they were the king's asshole.

Music was their love. They all wanted to be professional but in those days a recording contract was a voice from heaven. It was that rare. Not like now when you get a band together and hustle an advance. It was a closed shop.

Were you and Mick and Brian very strange for them?
That's right. They couldn't figure us out. Especially when I tried to lay Chuck Berry shit on them. "What are ya hangin' with them rock and rollers for?" they'd ask. Brian kicked a lot of them out and I really dug it. He turned around and said, "Fuck off, you bastards, you're a load of shit and I'm going to get it together with these cats." This cat Dick Taylor

shifted to bass by then. We were really looking for drums. Stew drifted with us for some reason. I sort of put him with those other cats because he had a job. But he said no too. "I'll stick around and see what happens with you."

So we got another back room in a different pub. Competition. Not that anybody came. Just rehearsin'.

Stew at that time used to turn up at rehearsals in a pair of shorts, on his bike. His piano used to be by the window and his biggest fear, the only thing that really stopped him at piano, was the thought that his bike might get nicked while he was playin'. So every now and then when someone walked past his bike, he'd stretch up and put his head out the window and keep playin', sit down again and then he'd see someone else lookin' at his bike. Up and up, still playin'.

Were you playing electric then?
Yeah. With homemade amps, old wireless sets. It took a while longer to get the electric bit together. At the time we thought, "Oh, it just makes it louder," but it ain't quite as simple at that.

Brian was the one who kept us all together then. Mick was still going to school. I'd dropped out. So we decided we got to live in London to get it together. Time to break loose. So everybody left home, upped and got this pad in London, Chelsea.

Different Chelsea than now?
Edith Grove. World's End. That place . . . every room got condemned slowly. It was like we slowly moved till we were all in the end room. Every room was shut up and stunk to hell, man. Terrible. Brian's only possession was a radio-record player. That, and a few beds and a little gas fire. We kept on playin', playin', playin'.

Brian kicked his job. He was in a department stare. He got into a very heavy scene for nickin' some bread and just managed to work his way out of it. So he thought, "Fuck it. If I work anymore I'm gonna get in real trouble." Get into jail or something.

He only nicked two pound . . . but he quit his job and his old lady had gone back to Cheltenham so he was on the loose again.

Are you gigging?

We didn't dare, man, we didn't dare. We were rehearsin' drummers. Mick Avory came by, the drummer of the Kinks. He was terrible, then. Couldn't find that off beat. Couldn't pick up on that Jimmy Reed stuff.

Is everybody still straight?

It was very hard to find anything. No one could afford to buy anything anyway. A little bit of grass might turn up occasionally but . . . everybody'd dig it . . . everybody's turn-on was just playing. It didn't matter if you were pissed. That was it. That was the big shot.

Mick was the only one who was still hovering because he was more heavily committed to the London School of Economics and he was being supported by a government grant, and his parents and all that. So he had a heavier scene to break away from than me because they were very pleased to kick me out anyway. And Brian too, they were glad to kick out. From university for making some chick pregnant or something.

Brian and I were the sort of people they were glad to kick out. They'd say, "You're nothing but bums, you're gonna end up on skid row," and that sort of thing. Probably will anyway. But Mick was still doing the two things. Brian and me'd be home in this pad all day tryin' to make one foray a day to either pick up some beer bottles from a party and sell 'em back for thruppence deposit or raid the local supermarket. Try and get some potatoes or some eggs or something.

I went out one morning and came back in the evening and Brian was *blowing harp*, man. He's got it together. He's standin' at the top of the stairs sayin', "Listen to this." *Whooooow. Whooow.* All these blues notes comin' out. "I've learned how to do it. I've figured it out." One day.

So then he started to really work on the harp. He dropped the guitar. He still dug to play it and was still into it and played very well but the harp became his thing. He'd walk around all the time playing his harp.

Is there anything going in London in terms of music then?

Alexis had that club together and we'd go down once a week to see what they were doing and they wanted to know what we were doing. "It's coming," we'd tell 'em. "We'll be gigging soon." We didn't know where the fuck do ya start? Where do ya go to play?

But you were living together, unlike Cyril Davies or the older blues musicians, because you were young and broke . . .
Yeah. Just Mick and myself and Brian. We knew Charlie. He was a friend. He was gigging at the time, playing with Alexis. He was Korner's drummer. We couldn't afford him.

One day we picked up a drummer called Tony Chapman who was our first regular drummer. Terrible. One of the worst . . . cat would start a number and end up either four times as fast as he started it or three times as slow. But never stay the same.

We did say, "Hey Tony, d'y'know any bass players?" He said, "I do know one." "Tell him come to next rehearsal." So we all turned up and in walks . . . Bill Wyman, ladies and gentleman. Huge speaker he's got, and a spare Vox eight-thirty amp which is the biggest amp we've ever seen in our lives. And that's spare. He says, "You can put one of your guitars through there." Whew. Put us up quite a few volts goin' through there.

He had the bass together already. He'd been playin' in rock bands for three or four years. He's older than us. He knows how to play. But he doesn't want to play with these shitty rock bands anymore because they're all terrible. They're all doing that Shadows trip, all those instrumental numbers, Duane Eddy, "Rebel Rouser." There was no one who could sing very good.

Also, they don't know what to play anymore. At that point, nobody wants to hear Buddy Holly anymore. He's an old scene already to the rock and roll hip circuit. It's that very light pop scene they're all into . . . Bobby Vee was a big scene then. You wouldn't dream of going to play in a ballroom. They'd just hurl bricks at you. Still have to stick to this little circuit of clubs, back rooms for one night, a shilling for everyone to get in. For people who didn't want to go to ballrooms. Who wanted to listen to something different.

Most of these clubs at the time are filled with dixieland bands, traditional jazz bands. An alternative to all that Bobby Vee stuff. There was a big boom in that: the stomp, stompin' about, weird dance, just really tryin' to break the ceiling to a two beat. That was the big scene. They had all the clubs under control. That's where Alexis made the breakthrough. He managed to open it up at the Ealing Club. Then he moved on to the Marquee and R&B started to become the thing. And all these traddies, as they were called, started getting worried. So they started this very bitter opposition.

Which is one reason I swung my guitar at Harold Pendleton's head at the Marquee thing, because he was the kingpin behind all that. He owned all these trad clubs and he got a cut from these trad bands, he couldn't bear to see them die. He couldn't afford it.

But Alexis was packin' em in man. Jus' playing blues. Very similar to Chicago stuff. Heavy atmosphere. Workers and art students, kids who couldn't make the ballrooms with supposedly long hair then, forget it, you couldn't go into those places. You gravitated to places where you wouldn't get hassled. The Marquee's a West End club, where we stood in for Alexis a couple of times.

With Charlie drumming?
No. Our first gig was down at the Ealing Club, a stand-in gig. That's the band without Charlie as drummer. We played everything. Muddy Waters. A lot of Jimmy Reed.

Still living in Chelsea?
Yeah. We had the middle floor. The top floor was sort of two school teachers tryin' to keep a straight life. God knows how they managed it. Two guys trainin' to be school teachers, they used to throw these bottle parties. All these weirdos, we used to think they were weirdos, they were as straight as . . . havin' their little parties up there, all dancing around to Duke Ellington. Then when they'd all zonked out, we'd go up there and nick all the bottles. Get a big bag, Brian and I, get all the beer bottles and the next day we'd take 'em to the pub to get the money on 'em.

Downstairs was livin' four old whores from Liverpool. Isn't that a coincidence. "'Allo dahlin', 'ow are ya? All right?" Real old boots they were. I don't know how they made their bread, working . . . They used to sort of nurse people and keep us together when we really got out of it.

The cat that supported Brian, this is a long story. He came from Brian's hometown. He got 80 quid a year for being in the Territorial Army in England, which is where you go for two weeks on a camp with the rest of these guys. Sort of a civil defense thing. They all live in tents and get soakin' wet and get a cold and at the end they learn how to shoot a rifle and they get 80 quid cash depending on what rank you've managed to wangle yourself.

This cat arrived in London with his 80 quid, fresh out of the hills, from his tent. And he wants to have a good time with Brian. And Brian took him for every penny, man. Got a new guitar. The whole lot.

This weird thing with this cat. He was one of those weird people who would do anything you say. Things like, Brian would say, "Give me your overcoat." Freezing cold, it's the worst winter and he gave Brian this Army overcoat. "Give Keith the sweater." So I put the sweater on.

"Now, you walk twenty yards behind us, man." And off we'd walk to the local hamburger place. "Ah, stay there. No, you can't come in. Give us two quid." Used to treat him like really weird. This cat would stand outside the hamburger joint freezing cold giving Brian the money to pay for our hamburgers. Never saw him again after that.

No, no, it ended up with us tryin' to electrocute him. It ended up with us gettin' out of our heads one night. That was the night he disappeared. It was snowing outside. We came back to our pad and he was in Brian's bed. Brian for some reason got very annoyed that he was in his bed asleep. We had all these cables lyin' around and he pulled out this wire. "This end is plugged in, baby, and I'm comin' after ya."

This cat went screaming out of the pad and into the snow in his underpants. "They're electrocuting me, they're electrocuting me." Somebody brought him in an hour later and he was blue. He was afraid to come in because he was so scared of Brian.

Brian used to pull these weird things. The next day the cat split. Brian had a new guitar, and his amp re-fixed, a whole new set of harmonicas.

I guess the craziness comes from the chemistry of the people. The craziness sort of kept us together. When the gigs become a little more plentiful and the kids started picking up on us was when we got picked up by Giorgio Gomelsky. Before he was into producing records. He was on the jazz club scene. I don't know exactly what he did, promoting a couple of clubs a week. He cottoned on to us and sort of organized us a bit.

We still didn't have Charlie as a drummer. We were really lacking a good drummer. We were really feeling it.

All I wanted to do is keep the band together. How we were going to do it and get gigs and people to listen to us? How to get a record together? We couldn't even afford to make a dub. Anyway we didn't have a drummer to make a dub with.

By this time we had it so together musically. We were really pleased with the way we were sounding. We were missing a drummer. We were missing good equipment. By this time the stuff we had was completely beaten to shit.

And the three of you get on? Are you the closest people for each other?
We were really a team. But there was always something between Brian, Mick and myself that didn't quite make it somewhere. Always something. I've often thought, tried to figure it out. It was in Brian, somewhere; there was something . . . he still felt alone somewhere . . . he was either completely into Mick at the expense of me, like nickin' my bread to go and have a drink. Like when I was zonked out, takin' the only pound I had in me pocket. He'd do something like that. Or he'd be completely in with me tryin' to work something against Mick. Brian was a very weird cat. He was a little insecure. He wouldn't be able to make it with two other guys at one time and really get along well.

I don't think it was a sexual thing. He was always so open with his chicks . . . It was something else I've never been able to figure out. You can read Jung. I still can't figure it out. Maybe it was in the stars. He was a Pisces. I don't know. I'm Sag and Mick's a Leo. Maybe those three can't ever connect completely all together at the same time for very long. There were periods when we had a ball together.

As we became more and more well-known and eventually grew into that giant sort of thing, that in Brian also became blown up until it became very difficult to work with and very difficult for him to be with us. Mick and I were more and more put together because we wrote together and Brian would become uptight about that because he couldn't write. He couldn't even ask if he could come and try to write something with us. Where earlier on Brian and I would sit for hours trying to write songs and say, "Aw fuck it, we can't write songs."

It worked both ways. When we played, it gave Brian ... man, when he wanted to play, he could play his ass off, that cat. To get him to do it, especially later on, was another thing. In the studio, for instance, to try and get Brian to play was such a hassle that eventually on a lot of those records that people think are the Stones, it's me overdubbing three guitars and Brian zonked out on the floor.

It became very difficult because we were working non-stop ... I'm skipping a lot of time now ... when we were doing those American tours in '64, '65, '66. When things were getting really difficult. Brian would go out and meet a lot of people, before we did, because Mick and I spent most of our time writing. He'd go out and get high somewhere, get smashed. We'd say, "Look, we got a session tomorrow, man, got to keep it together." He'd come, completely out of his head, and zonk out on the floor with his guitar over him. So we started overdubbing, which was a drag cause it meant the whole band wasn't playing.

Can you tell me about Oldham?
Andrew had the opportunity. He didn't have the talent, really. He didn't have the talent for what he wanted to be. He could hustle people and there's nothing wrong with hustling ... it still has to be done to get through. You need someone who can talk for you. But he's got to be straight with you too.

Was he in the business before the Stones?
Yeah, he was with the Beatles. He helped kick them off in London. Epstein hired him and he did a very good job for them. One doesn't know how much of a job was needed but he managed to get them a lot of space in the press when "Love Me Do" came out and was like number nine in the charts and the kids were turning on to them and it was obvious they were going to be big, big, because they were only third on the bill and yet they were tearing the house down every night. A lot of it was down to Andrew. He got them known. And he did the same gig for us. He did it. Except he was more involved with us. He was working for us.

He had a genius for getting things through the media. Before people really knew what media was, to get messages through without people knowing.

Anita: But Brian, he never got on with Andrew.

Keith: Never. I've seen Brian and Andrew really pissed hanging all over each other but really basically there was no chemistry between them. They just didn't get on. There was a time when Mick and I got on really well with Andrew. We went through the whole *Clockwork Orange* thing. We went through that whole trip together. Very sort of butch number. Ridin' around with that mad criminal chauffeur of his.

Epstein and Oldham did a thing on the media in England that's made it easier for millions of people since and for lots of musicians. It's down to people like those that you can get on a record now. They blew that scene wide open, that EMI-Decca stranglehold. EMI is still the biggest record company in the whole fucking world despite being an English company. They can distribute in Hong Kong. They have it sewn up in the Philippines and Australia and everywhere. No matter who you go through, somewhere in the world, EMI is dealing your records. It's a network left over from the colonial days and they've kept hold of it.

Oldham made money for the Stones.
Yeah. I mean, God knows how much money has been made on the Stones name and how much of it has got through to us and how much got through to people along the way. Without mentioning any names but there is one guy I'm still going to get.

It's not money. It's like, what do you want? And how do you want to get it? And do you want to keep it cool? It's not simple, cut and dried. By the time it goes through all those peoples' hands they're pretty soiled those dollar bills. To work it out any other way, you have to end up like them to do it.

How long was Andrew involved?
From '63 to the end of '67. It still goes on though. I got a letter the other day about some litigation, Oldham versus Eric Easton, who was our first

manager proper. Oldham was only half of the team, the other was Eric Easton, who was just a bumbly old Northern agent. Handled a couple semi-successful chick singers and could get you gigs in ball rooms in the North of England. Once it got to America, this cat Easton dissolved. He went into a puddle. He couldn't handle that scene.

Was Charlie drumming with you when Andrew first saw you work?
I'll tell you how we picked Charlie up. I told you about the people Brian was getting a band together with and then he turned on to us and he told those other people to fuck off, et cetera. Our common ground with Brian back then was Elmore James and Muddy Waters. We laid Slim Harpo on him, and Fred McDowell.

Because Brian was from Cheltenham, a very genteel town full of old ladies, where it used to be fashionable to go and take the baths once a year at Cheltenham Spa. The water is very good because it comes out of the hills, it's spring water. It's a Regency thing, you know Beau Brummel, around that time. Turn of the 19th century. Now it's a seedy sort of place full of aspirations to be an aristocratic town. It rubs off on anyone who comes from there.

The R&B thing started to blossom and we found playing on the bill with us in a club, there were two bands on, Charlie was in the other band. He'd left Korner, and was with the same cats Brian had said fuck off to about six months before. We did our set and Charlie was knocked out by it. "You're great, man," he says, "but you need a fucking good drummer." So we said, "Charlie, we can't afford you, man." Because Charlie had a job and just wanted to do weekend gigs. Charlie used to play anything then—he'd play pubs, anything, just to play, cause he loves to play with good people. But he always had to do it for economic reasons. By this time we're getting three, four gigs a week. "Well, we can't pay you as much as that band but . . ." we said. So he said, OK and told the other band to fuck off, "I'm gonna play with these guys."

That was it. When we got Charlie, that really made it for us. We started getting a lot of gigs. Then we got that Richmond gig with Giorgio and that built up to an enormous scene. In London, that was *the* place to be every

Sunday night. At the Richmond Station Hotel. It's on the river Richmond, a fairly well-to-do neighborhood but kids from all over London would come down there on a Sunday night.

There's only so far you can go on that London scene; if you stay in that club circuit eventually you get constipated. You go round and round so many times and then suddenly, you're not the hip band anymore, someone else is. Like the High Numbers, they took over from us in a lot of clubs. The High Numbers turned out to become the Who. The Yardbirds took over from us in Richmond and on Sunday nights we'd find we were booked into a place in Manchester.

Where are you recording now, with Giorgio?
Not with Giorgio. Eric and Andrew fucked Giorgio because he had nothing on paper with us. They screwed him to get us a recording contract. We were saying to Giorgio, "What about records?" and he didn't have it together for the record thing. Not for a long time afterwards either. He was still very much a club man. We knew that to go any further and reach out a bit, we wanted to get off the club thing and get into the ballrooms where the kids were. It turned out to be right.

It was difficult the first few months though. We were known in the big cities but when you get outside into the sticks, they don't know who the fuck you are and they're still preferring the local band. That makes you play your ass off every night so that at the end of two hour-long sets, you've got 'em. You've gotta do it. That's the testing ground, in those ballrooms where it's really hard to play.

Stew is driving you around now?
Yeah, there was this whole thing, because for us Stew is one of the band up until Andrew. "Well, he just doesn't look the part," Andrew said, "and six is too many for them to remember the faces in the picture." But piano is important for us. Brian at that time is the leader of the band. He pulled us all together, he's playing good guitar, but his love is the harmonica. On top of that, he's got the pop star hangup—he wants to sing, with Mick, like "Walking the Dog."

Are you singing?

Naw, I was getting into writing then though. Andrew was getting on to me
to write because he sussed that maybe I could do it if I put my mind to it.

What are some of the first things you wrote?

They're on the first album. "Tell Me," which was pulled out as a single
in America, which was a dub. Half those records were dubs on that first
album, that Mick and I and Charlie and I'd put a bass on or maybe Bill
was there and he'd put a bass on. "Let's put it down while we remember
it" and the next thing we know is, "Oh look, track eight is that dub we did
a couple months ago." That's how little control we had, we were driving
around the country every fucking night, playing a different gig, sleeping
in the van, hotels if we were lucky.

A lot of it was Andrew's choice. He selected what was to be released.
He was executive record producer, so-called. While we were gigging, he'd
get that scene together. But remember then, it was important to put out a
single every three months. You had to put out a 45, a red-hot single, every
three months. An album was something like Motown—you put the hit
single on the album and ten tracks of shit and then rush it out. Now, the
album is the thing. Marshall has laid the figures on me and *Sticky Fingers*
album has done more than the single. They're both number one in the
charts but the album's done more than the single.

The concept's changed so completely. Back then it was down to turning on 13-year-old chicks and putting out singles every three months.
That was the basic force of the whole business. That was how it was done.

That's another thing. Both the Beatles and us had been through buy-
ing albums that were filled with ten tracks of rubbish. We said, "No, we
want to make each track good. Work almost as hard on it as you would
work on a single." So maybe we changed that concept.

Still, we were on the road every night so there are probably a couple
of tracks in there that are probably bummers because Andrew said, "Well,
put that on." Because up until the Beatles and ourselves got into records,
the cat who was singing had absolutely no control, man. None at all. He
had no say in the studio. The backing track was laid down by session men,

under the A and R man, artists and repertoire, whatever the fuck that means. He controlled the artist and the material. Bobby Vee or Billy Fury just laid down the vocal. They weren't allowed to go into the booth and say, "I want my voice to sound like this or I want the guitar to sound like this." The man from the record company decided what went where.

That's why there became longer and longer gaps between albums coming out because we got into trying to make everything good.

The first three albums are pretty close though.
The first one was done all in England. In a little demo studio in "Tin Pan Alley" as it used to be called. Denmark Street in Soho. It was all done on a two-track Revox that he had on the wall. We used to think, "Oh, this is a recording studio, huh? This is what they're like?" A tiny little backroom.

When we got into RCA in Hollywood, fuckin' huge Studio A, with Dave Hassinger engineering we said, "We can really do it here. It's all laid out. All you have to do is not let them take you over." Engineers never even used to work, man. They'd flick a few switches and that was it. The machinery was unsophisticated in those days, four track was the biggest there was.

Suddenly a whole new breed of engineers appears, like Glyn Johns, people who are willing to work with you, and not with someone from the record company. There are all those weird things which have broken up in the record industry, which haven't happened for movies yet. There are no more in between men between you and the engineer and you can lay it down. If you want a producer or feel you need one, which most people do, it's a close friend, someone you dig to work with, that translates for you. Eventually we found Jimmy Miller, after all those years.

Slowly and slowly, we've been finding the right people to do the right thing like Marshall Chess, like Jo Bergman. All those people are as important as we are. Especially now that we've got Rolling Stones records, with the Kali tongue . . . nobody's gotten into that yet, but that's Kali, the Hindu female goddess. Five arms, a row of heads around her, a sabre in one hand, flames coming out the other, she stands there, with her tongue out. But that's gonna change. That symbol's not going to stay as it is. Sometimes it'll take up the whole label, maybe slowly it'll turn to a cock, I don't know yet.

You going to put two pills on the tongue?
We're going to do everything with it, slowly. Don't want to let it grow stale. It's growing change. Got to keep it growing.

What was the first time Oldham saw the band?
It was in March, 1963. The next week he took us right into a big studio and we cut "Come On." We were always doing other people's material but we thought we'd have a go at that—"Oh, it sounds catchy." And it worked out. At the time it was done just to get a record out. We never wanted to hear it. The idea was Andrew's—to get a strong single so they'd let us make an album which back then was a privilege.

Were you still a London band then?
Completely. We'd never been out of the city. I'd never been further north than the north of London.

Was Andrew a change in the kind of people you had to deal with?
He faced us with the real problems. That we had to find the hole to get out of the circle of London clubs and into the next circle. Lot of hustle, a lot of blague.

Did you have an image thing already?
It's funny. He tried . . . people think Oldham made the image, but he tried to tidy us up. He fought it. Absolutely. There are photographs of us in suits he put us in, those dog-tooth checked suits with the black velvet collars. Everybody's got black pants, and a tie and a shirt. For a month on the first tour, we said, "All right. We'll do it. You know the game. We'll try it out." But then the Stones thing started taking over. Charlie'd leave his jacket in some dressing room and I'd pull mine out and there'd be whiskey stains all over it or chocolate pudding. The thing just took over and by the end of the tour we were playing in our own gear again because that's all we had left. Which was the usual reason.

You weren't the socially "smart" band yet?
No. The Beatles went through it, and they put us through it. They have to

know you. They've changed a lot too you know. A lot of them have gone through some funny trips. Some titled gentlemen of some stature are now roaming around England like gypsies and they've acquired this fantastic country Cockney accent. "Ai sole a fe 'orses down 'ere. Got a new caravan like and we're thinking of tripping up to see . . ." But it's great.

It must have been amazing early on, when some young lord or some young titled lady would come to see you play?
Brian and I were really fascinated by them. They used to make us really laugh, from a real working class thing. It was so silly to us. It happened so fast that one never had time to really get into that thing, "Wow, I'm a Rolling Stone." We were still sleeping in the back of this truck every night because of the most hard-hearted and callous roadie I've ever encountered, Stew. From one end of England to another in Stew's Volkswagen bus. With just an engine and a rear window and all the equipment and then you fit in. The gear first though.

But to even get out of London then was such a weird trip for Mick and me. The North. Like we went back this year right, on the English tour, and it hasn't changed a bit, man. In the Thirties, it used to look exactly the same, in the middle of the depression. It's never ended for those people.

You're travelling alone?
Sure. Never carry chicks. Pick it up there or drop it. No room, man. Stew wouldn't allow it. Crafty Bill Wyman. For years we believed that he couldn't travel in the back of the bus or he'd spew all over us so he was always allowed to sit in the passenger seat. Years later, we find out he never gets travel sick at all.

Is the first album out?
No, we released two singles before the album. The first single was "Come On" with Muddy Waters' "I Wanna Be Loved" on the other side. We were learning to record. Andrew too. He'd never made a record in his life, and he was producing. Just to walk in and start telling people, it took guts. Andrew had his own ideas on what we were supposed to sound like. It's only been in the last few years with Jimmy that it's changed. The music went through Andrew then. He was in the booth.

Was there a period when it was all the same, just working, but you knew something was building?

It's weird. I can remember. You know it in front. Being on the road every night you can tell by the way the gigs are going, there's something enormous coming. You can feel this energy building up as you go around the country. You feel it winding tighter and tighter, until one day you get out there halfway through the first number and the whole stage is full of chicks screaming "Nyeehhh." There was a period of six months in England we couldn't play ballrooms anymore because we never got through more than three or four songs every night, man. Chaos. Police and too many people in the places, fainting.

We'd walk into some of those places and it was like they had the Battle of the Crimea going on, people gasping, tits hanging out, chicks choking, nurses running around with ambulances.

I know it was the same for the Beatles. One had been reading about that, "Beatlemania." "Scream power" was the thing everything was judged by, as far as gigs were concerned. If Gerry and the Pacemakers were the top of the bill, incredible, man. You know that weird sound that thousands of chicks make when they're really lettin' it go. They couldn't hear the music. We couldn't hear ourselves, for years. Monitors were unheard of. It was impossible to play as a band on stage, and we forgot all about it.

Did you develop a stage act?

Not really. Mick did his thing and I tried to keep the band together. That's always what it's been, basically. If I'm leapin' about, it's only because something's goin' drastically wrong or it's going drastically right.

Mick had always dug visual artists himself. He always loved Diddley and Chuck Berry and Little Richard for the thing they laid on people on stage. He really dug James Brown the first time he saw him. All that organization . . . ten dollar fine for the drummer if he missed the off beat.

What was Brian like onstage?

He'd worked out these movements. In those days, little chicks would all have their favorites. Yeah, when you think the Rolling Stones magazine, the Beatles magazine came out once a month. Big sort of fan thing. It was a very old thing that one had the feeling had to change. All those teenyboppers.

It might have been a great last gasp.
Yeah, I think so. Chicks now maybe they feel more equal. I think chicks and guys have gotten more into each other, realized there's the same in each. Instead of them having to go through that completely hysterical, completely female trip to let it out that way. Probably now they just screw it out.

Was it innocent hysteria?
They used to tell us, "There's not a dry seat in the cinema." It was like that.

Were you being approached by the kids?
Yeah, I got strangled twice. That's why I never wear anything around my neck any more. Going out of theatres was the dodgiest. One chick grabs one side of the chain and another chick grabs the other side . . . Another time I found myself lying in the gutter with shirt on and half a pair of pants and the car roaring away down the street. Oh shit, man. They leap on you. "What do you want? What?"

You have to get a little crazy from that.
You get completely crazy. And the bigger it got, America and Australia and everywhere it's exactly the same number. Oh, we were so glad when that finished. We stopped. We couldn't go on anymore. And when we decided to get it together again, everybody had changed.

Was it the same kind of madness in the States before it changed?
Completely different kind of madness. Before, America was a real fantasy land. It was still Walt Disney and hamburger dates, and when you came back in 1969 it wasn't anymore. Kids were really into what was going on in their country. I remember watching Goldwater-Johnson in '64 and it was a complete little show. But by the time it came to Nixon's turn two years ago, people were concerned in a really different way.

Rock music as politics?
Who knows, man? I mean they used to try and put it down so heavy, rock 'n' roll. I wonder if they knew there was some rhythm in there that

Shortly after a purple scarf is placed on the drum podium the lights go down and the band walks out. A spot picks out Keith as he cranks up the intro to "Honky Tonk Women" and then BLAM! It's loud, it's awesome, it's the Greatest Rock and Roll Band In The World!

The band stands still, working the music, leaving Jagger out front to pout and swagger, shimmy and blow kisses and do all those Jagger things. The stage is a masterpiece in white, which the band slowly starts to use in their various stage roles of running, jumping, standing still. The sound is dreadful, at first all rhythm, then painful slabs of trebly guitar. Jagger works really hard at being Jagger, interspersed with showbiz *shtick* that we've never before seen in rock and roll: manhandling a dragon, fighting a huge blow-up penis that half-heartedly erupts from the stage floor, swinging on a rope. It's ok, but it doesn't look cool until you see it frozen in photos. Do the Stones think that playing the world's most dangerous music is no longer enough?

The old hits remind us why we're alive; the new, ordinary songs from *Black and Blue* pull us back from Olympus. Jagger talks to us, prods us— "C'mon Frankfurt!"—trying to find the magic thread in an off night, but he does it using a preposterous Negro accent and the unwanted thought creeps into view that, really, the singer is a bit of a tosser.

They end with the crowd pleasers of "Jumping Jack Flash" and "Street Fighting Man," played fast and messy. Then, in the midst of the noise is a huge out of tune twang and Keith is . . . let Charlie Murray describe it: "You know the riffs: that when Keith Richard comes into the room rock and roll walks in the door. Yeah, well rock and roll just fell on its arse." Mick looks back and with an *"oh dear"* expression minces over, swooping on the move to pick up the dropped plectrum and hand it to Keith, who is sitting with splayed legs, hammering away with his fingers.

We are ushered into Keith and Ron's suite—large, high-ceilinged, matching bodyguards at the door. In the centre an open flight case holds two Fender amplifiers. A cassette deck on top of one playing Furry Lewis, Robert Johnson, Burning Spear. In a corner Ron lounges on an ornate couch. Against the wall on the other side Keith holds court with a group of journalists and I kneel on the floor directly to his right. The chair looks like a throne and he's draped over it like discarded clothes, holding in his right hand a foot long slab of turquoise, flat on the upper surface and jagged on the underside. If he puts it down it will tip over and spill the contents of the flat side, which he's not going to because it holds what looks like a Himalayan range of cocaine. It's a dull, flat white powder—pharmaceutical cocaine, almost impossible to get, manufactured just down the autobahn in the Swiss laboratories of Merck AG.

While he talks he twirls a small square of neatly cut cardboard, using it to cut fastidious lines out from the mountain range and then, using a silver tube on a silver chain around his neck, casually snort them up between sentences. We're there for 30?, 45?, 90? minutes. In this room someone has pushed Time's pause button. So ask a question; Keith will answer.

"Too much technology makes it more and more difficult to record rock and roll properly <*snff!*> In Russia they spend so many rubles on black market records and there's a very big scene in South America but when you try to do a tour there there's so many problems <*snff!*> I miss singles but there's not a singles market anymore <*snff!*> We never sat down to write singles, we sat down to write songs <*slice, chop, shape*> I never listen to white bands because white drummers don't swing, except for Charlie Watts."

While Keith talks the mountain range in his hand becomes a mountain, a hill, a bump, a dusty memory. Nothing seems to change: his speech remains slow and relaxed, his body flops like tomorrow's washing and he sounds coherent. Only the half-baked thinking betrays him. And just when you think, God he's boring, he'll say:

"I was reading a history of Bill Broonzy nicked from Hendon Library the other day and there was a little bit there where he said that if he were to put a band together again he'd have pot smokers instead of drinkers. They don't forget their notes and they're on time."

Suddenly there's a frisson of excitement. Another pile of cocaine is on the slab, Swiss Alps–sized this time (an appropriate metaphor given the persistent rumour that every six months he gets his blood changed there), and he's neatly parcelling out eight even lines. And there are eight people around him . . . Keith is going to get us high! Now if there's one immutable truth in this palace of self-centredness it's that Keith Richards is not going to share his drugs with a bunch of journalists and sure enough, as he <*snff!*> continues to talk he <*snff!*> casually snorts <*snff!*> all eight lines.

Charles ambles over, kneels on the floor and licks Rizzlas. Naturally, Keith chats to his new friend until Ron walks over to hold a card in front of Keith, on which is scrawled: "You're talking to Charles Shaar Murray."

With a show of boneyard teeth Keith challenges, "Your review was rubbish."

Charles calmly rubs thick crumbs of black hashish into the waiting Silk Cut. "I stand by what I wrote."

"You need to hear it again."

"That's ok, most of my friends think it's awful as well."

"You need to widen your circle of friends."

It's bizarre to watch this schoolboy bickering—a rock god trading insults with a critic. As if our opinions *mattered*.

Charles has a smoke and passes it to Keith. When he hands it to me it's a roach. Keith is defending *Black and Blue*, but no explanation can redeem it. Indeed, the story that it was assembled during 1974 and 1975 as an audition for guitarists to replace Mick Taylor damns it further. It's just released and it's already over a year old—rock and roll is about next week. Tellingly, the cover photo is by a celebrity snapper-du-jour, the first time the Stones have followed fashion instead of leading it.

For some months I have been following four urchins busy working out what rock and roll in the Seventies should sound like and this seems the right time to speak up. "Keith, there's a band in London called the Sex Pistols." He looks bored. "They think you're old and should stop playing and get out of the way." He jerks forward, ultrasheen eyes glaring and just below the surface a volcano is erupting.

"Just let them try," he snarls, jabbing the joint at me. "We're the Rolling Stones. No-one tells us what to do. We'll stop when we feel like it." Emotion spent, he sinks back into his throne, realises he's holding a roach and passes it to me.

Indefinably, a wave of charisma washes through the room. In the doorway stands Mick Jagger. He is stationary, hands on narrow hips, head slightly tilted and looking up, the King ready to acknowledge our worship. Only everyone looks up, thinks, "Oh right, Mick," and goes back to what they're doing. His shoulders slump and he stalks over to the couch. No one goes over to him. In our journalistic japery we've assigned them roles like some cliché vaudeville gang; one critic had said earlier, "Who gives a shit what Mick Jagger thinks about these days?", and it seems to be true.

But we do care what Keith thinks and as he tells us he wipes his nose with a finger and scrapes it off on his trouser leg. A foot from my eyes, stuck to the corduroy, is a thick line of cocaine mixed with a little snot and for a mad punk minute I think of leaning forward and with a quick "Excuse me Keith," snorting it. But manners prevail and I wonder how much more pharmaceutical-grade powder is lodged undissolved in his nose.

Charles is now on the couch sharing a joint with Ron while Mick broods next to them. Cutting through their talk come the distinct Jagger tones, now clothed in Cockney, "I fort your review was blaahdy stoopid." Charles ignores him and Mick repeats himself. Same result. Mick sulks, then gets up and talks to a mountainesque heavy, who in turn talks to a record company man and then it is announced: we must leave. Charles is now building joint number four and continues work while we're shepherded out. Keith follows.

"Jagger," he sneers with contempt, "wants to go over a few songs and change things around. But later on we'll go up to Billy's room. There's going to be a party."

He waits and chats while the joint is finished and the touch paper lit. Charles savours his work with a connoisseur's appreciation, watching the smoke exhalations, small-talking to Keith, having another draw, finally handing it to Keith, who opens the door, backs through it and with a cheery "See you later," waves the incriminating hand and shuts the door.

Three weeks later, the Stones start their first English tour since 1973. Driving to London after a show in Stafford, Keith drives his Bentley off the road. As the press jubilantly report, the police search his car, find "a substance," arrest and then release him on bail while forensics determine what it, "obviously a drug" according to the police, might be.

Their canter into London for six nights at Earls Court triggers press adulation. Hold the front page—MICK IS A GODFATHER! MICK MEETS PRINCESS MARGARET! Every night sees a private party, from pubs to Sothebys. And Ron Wood has his salary held while Deltapad, a management company, sues Promotone Productions over causing Ron to breach contract by playing with friends. A few miles away in a crummy club, fifty people watch a scrappy group called the Sex Pistols work on a sound to change the world.

6 |

NO ONE SHOT KR: KEITH RICHARDS 1980

KRIS NEEDS | 1980

This interview with Richards was conducted at a point between the negligible but high-charting *Emotional Rescue* and *Tattoo You*, which though mostly composed of dolled-up discards would transpire to be the final landmark Rolling Stones album. Already perceived by many as over-the-hill or even betrayers of a generation's ideals, the Stones were assuming a curious simultaneous position of irrelevant and commercially colossal.

As such, this would be just about the final time Richards could command a cover of an alternative publication like *Zigzag*. Yet, even at this point, *Zigzag* would probably not have put Mick Jagger on its cover. The street cred Richards still retained derived partly from his outlaw image, which had been underlined by a 1977 Toronto drug bust that saw him theoretically face a life sentence for heroin trafficking. With his eventual suspended sentence partly dependent on cleaning up, a smack-free Richards was now at liberty to talk completely candidly about the drug for the first time.

When this piece first appeared, some columns were pasted in the incorrect order. The author has now corrected the resultant sequential mistakes so that more than three decades down the line the feature is appearing for the first time the way it was originally intended to be published.

Note: for "MacLagen" read "McLagan."

for "Pallenburg" read "Pallenberg."

One Saturday evening in 1963 an eight-year-old perched on a chair, peepers glued to a small wooden telly. Wheezing out of the tube was "Thank

Your Lucky Stars," the now-extinct weekly showcase for Pop Stars of the day. The wide-eyed Beatles rubbed Rickenbackers with heart-throbs like Cliff, Dusty and Pat Boone. Safe for kiddies.

This particular Saturday a new sensation came bursting through the cleancut cuties. Five shaggy unknowns called the Rolling Stones, ill-fitting suits a reluctant compromise, bowled on and savaged the nation's blood pressure with raw, wailing blues.

That was it. I was grabbed. Watched every TV appearance, devoured the records and sowed all the seeds of what I still believe as the Stones carved a chaotic swathe through convention and petty values. I didn't wear me cap to school cos I knew Brian Jones wouldn't and revelled in the effect liking the Stones had on Beatles-fan friends. Cheered 'em through the court cases and finally saw me first gig at the 1968 NME Poll-winners concert.

Gradually sheer fan-fixation grew into total addiction to the monumental music they steered us into the 70s with.

The pre-and-early-teen me thought Jagger was The Man. But by "Beggars Banquet" and "Let It Bleed" it'd dawned that the entire Stones thing now laid square on the spikey head of Keith Richards. If Charlie Watts was the engine room, Keith was the machine and its inventor, whipping up the body-riffs with that churning guitar.

Amidst all the gloss and pompous irrelevance of the early 70s, here was this geezer who didn't care so long as he could play and live the way he wanted.

I saw him persecuted and prosecuted as they tried to do a Brian Jones and batter him into the ground with litigation. Doing a Houdini out of all that by cleaning up the bad eggs, Richards then found himself taking the Stones through a flakbarrage of punk (Ironic seeing's a lot of 'em merely took old Stones blueprints and speeded 'em up!).

The Stones were charged with everything—irrelevance, old age, being jet-setting tax exiles, dinosaurs . . . dirt. But the records still sold, even though some of the recent stuff ain't matched up to Stones-scratch—blame that on pressures and growing apart as Keith Richards fights to get it down fast and out, the feeling intact (with ballsups), while Mick Jagger polishes away. Compromise can stifle and it riddled "Emotional Rescue," but they can still shine (and I know who's on *that* particular case).

This interview took years to come and was in reach for months before Keith was in the right place and right mind. He's really gone off interviews, you see.

We met at his hotel but had to go to the Stones office in Chelsea—a ten-minute drive . . .

"Oops, I'm going the wrong way," remarks Mr Richards. "I'll have to do a U-turn!" The big blue Rent-A-Merc curves across three lanes and he blows kisses at the surprised motorists going home from work.

We end up talking for nearly three hours. Keith would spout about anything in his slow, deliberate, laugh-peppered croak. He talked a bit like his driving, going where the bourbon-fuelled thought patterns took him.

The 1980 model Keith Richards is devoid of Rock Star flash, maturing like a caring, kindly old blues musician. But he still possesses an indefinable swagger that makes any of the preening idiots that still profess to be R 'n' R stars look the pathetic buffoons they really are. In a grey RAF sweater too!

Talk kicks off: Jack Daniels in hands and my fags going fast. The ailing Music Biz and its Major companies provides a jumping off point.

KR: . . . I think they're squealing like fat pigs—there weren't as much in the trough this year as they expected. No way is the record business declining, it just ain't growing as fast as they'd all got used to expecting. You know—30 per cent more in America almost every year for the last few years. Suddenly they only get 20 per cent more so they start squealing and start axing everybody and giving the artists a hard time. "Aw, I was going to buy a new Rolls Royce this year and now I can't afford it because we're only 20 per cent up and not 30 per cent up on business," and they start screaming "Recession!" use that as an excuse, come down heavy on the musicians.

ZZ: It hasn't really hit you lot though, has it?
KR: No, since we have our own label they turn round and think "oh you've got a label, you're one of us." Bullshit, man! We're not. We're just gonna do what we do anyway. It don't affect us that much, at least not noticeably. We're still gonna try and get this label off the ground slowly. Apart from just ourselves, Peter Tosh has done real well, much better than anyone expected . . . he's just broken in South America real big. He did these

big festivals down there and suddenly we're getting this demand for Peter Tosh records and we ain't got 'em! Factory didn't press enough.

ZZ: Anyone else coming out?
KR: Yeah . . . Earl McGrath, who's been running the label for us found this good white kid from New York called Jim Carroll. I did a couple of numbers with him in New York but I was drunk so "yeah alright!" Actually Mick was supposed to join me but he chickened out at the last minute. Cunt. That album should be out soon. We haven't got enough staff to work on more than one album at a time, so they're waiting until they don't have to do as much work on "Emotional Rescue" or whatever, and when that's over they'll put out Jim Carroll's album. I heard it a couple of times—he's good, and he gets better cos he cut the album once a couple of years ago, and I said you should do some gigs for a year and think about it again. So they recut it after a year of working, and it's a good record. It's a fairly basic sound, he uses his voice kinda like Lou Reed, almost half-talking. He'd written a couple of books before he started writing songs so there's some good lyrics.

ZZ: And you've got another Stones album coming from the "Emotional Rescue" sessions, you said earlier.
KR: Yeah, they sent me six C90 cassettes full of stuff, not all finished, but ideas for songs, a few demos, here and there and a surprising amount of finished stuff, a lot of instrumentals. Some of the stuff went back into the Mid-70s, stuff with Billy Preston just jamming, riffs . . . but there's an album there, although we'll probably put a basic album together and see what we need to finish it off. Then we might go in and record for a couple of weeks to cut a couple of new ones, to add.

ZZ. When "Emotional Rescue" came out there were a lot of disgruntled "oh it's taken them two years to do this"—type criticisms.
KR: They're quite right in a way. Having so much stuff, we've just had songs coming out of our ears lately. Also you do write quite a lot of songs in two years—try 'em out. Some songs actually take a couple of years to get out of the mind and onto tape. You try it three or four different ways

over a few months and it doesn't quite work, and then one day later someone says, "remember that one?" and you remember it slightly differently
and you get it in one, things like that.

ZZ: So were you happy with what eventually came out?
KR: Yeah, I mean it's almost as bad as not having enough—not quite,
that's the worst feeling (laughs)—but having a lot it takes so long cos
you've gotta listen to everything you've got and that takes up a load of
time because you've got so much stuff. Then you cut that down to a short
list, eventually get it down to album length as far as songs go, and then
start editing them down, cos some are too long. That album's not by any
means the best of the stuff that we did, not like, "that was the best and this
album's the second best of what we've got." It's just, up to a point, what
was ready and what we could finish in time, because it had to be ready by
March or April or whatever it was.

Keith's track, "All about You" was unanimously lambasted when "Emotional Rescue" came out, but it stands out as one of the moments of real
emotion on the record. Unfortunately it seems that Mick Jagger has
slipped to trotting out mainly superficial parodies of himself or other artists (the Bee Gees on the title track, boozy punk on "Where the Boys Go",
etc.). Meanwhile Keith's contributions can be traced through the years as
sources of genuine raw feeling: "You Got the Silver" ("Let It Bleed"), his
strained attack on "Happy" ("Exile"), the pained "Comin' Down Again"
("Goats Head Soup"), the stumbling "Harder They Come," "Run Rudolph
Run," most recently "All About You." Though the guitar never falters, the
voice cracks, but it's from the heart not the wallet or the ego. "All about
You" is an aching but bitter love song, Keith slurring and whining a put-
down. But any stereotyped sexist jibes are dispelled by the last line's, "how
come I'm still in love with you." A million miles more real than "she might
be the alien."

ZZ: "All about You" is my personal favourite.
KR: (Seeming a mite taken aback) Ah good . . . hur! (short laugh). I enjoyed
doing it. That was another of them songs which must've been around for

three years, maybe even a bit more. I wrote it in some soundcheck, Charlie was keeping time. I was convinced myself because it came so easy, the actual basic song—"this is someone else's song and I can't remember what it is." For ages I was hawking this tape and saying "who's is this" and they go, "uh hold on . . . um . . ." Nobody could put their fingers on it so after three years I thought, "well . . . I must have written it!" So I went ahead and finished the lyrics and that.

ZZ: It sounds like you sat there at the piano when everybody had gone home and plonked it out then added the horns and stuff later. . .
KR: When we eventually cut the track and put the horns on it last year I still wasn't entirely convinced exactly how it should go, so I had the track and everybody was saying, "you've got a song to put on it then we should put it on the album." But I still hadn't written it. Then, as you said, everybody went home and I sat down by the microphone and started it on the spot. [I] hadn't written anything for it, I just started doing it and after two or three hours started to take shape. I put harmonies on it . . . although when I was doing it I still wasn't thinking necessarily of me singing it, I was just sort of writing it and doing it to keep it for myself to remember how it went, and to play it to Mick if he wanted to do it. But when it was finished everyone said it should stay like that so I said fine, okay.

ZZ: You sound pissed!
KR: . . . (chuckles) yeah. I didn't try to clean it up, if I'd tried to change it I'd have probably screwed it up. I like it as it is.

ZZ:. I read about some conflict between you wanting a raw sound on the album and Mick wanting to clean it all up . . .
KR: Well . . . I always get a bit obstinate, 'specially towards him when I think "'Christ, we've been working on this thing nearly two years and if I don't watch it it's not gonna come out unless I start kicking the fuckin' walls down and stuff.'" But that happens. with every album . . . (laughs). You ain't gonna get through two years in the studio without somebody getting shirty.

ZZ: What tracks did you have most to do with on that album then?
KR: Er . . . Eventually all of 'em, but I had more to do with . . . obviously "All about You," "She's So Cold," "Let Me Go" . . . Fffff . . . gimme some tracks, what else is on there?

ZZ: "Where the Boys Go"?
KR: "Where the Boys Go," yeah. That was a real band effort, it was Mick's song, and "Summer Romance," but we'd played 'em a lot. Pretty much everybody was into those. "Indian Girl" was Mick cos I just played piano on that. I enjoyed doing something different. "Send It to Me" and "Emotional Rescue" are both Mick's songs but we all worked on the tracks.

ZZ: I thought "Send It to Me" was pretty lightweight when you consider the Stones' deep immersion in reggae (and Keith playing so well on corkers like "Shine Eye").
KR: There you get on another of my beefs on the making of this album: alright you got ten tracks, but it's the first one in two years and I thought "Emotional Rescue" and "Send It to Me" were just a little too similar—not necessarily musically, just in the sound—that mid-tempo sort of . . . I just thought we were giving a lot of plastic vinyl over to a very similar sound and I was saying, "You should have one or the other of those two—then you could put a couple of other tracks on, couple of other rockers that we had almost ready. But I gave that one up: 'Cos originally "Dance" had a whole vocal thing, it was swamped with vocals. Mick had decided he'd got to write this song to this track. He did a lot of work on it and he did a good job, but it *totally* nullified the track. I said "let's make it an instru[mental', to which he replied,] 'I can't waste time on an album with only ten tracks and instrumentals' . . . instrumentals have got a dirty name. Everyone thinks it's just a filler, but some of the best rock 'n' roll records I can remember are instrumentals—Johnny and the Hurricanes, the Ventures, Bill Black's Combo . . . instrumentals used to be a regular part of your diet. *We* used to put out instrumentals from the very first album —"'Now I've Got a Witness'"—just let a band have a blow once in a while. Sometimes you can screw a track up by putting a vocal on it, you lose some of its impact cos it's neither a song and it's no longer an instrumental.

ZZ: Also I heard Bill left for a couple of months while it was being done.
KR: I dunno. He said something about retiring to somebody and then he got a new manager, but Bill, as far back as I can remember, is never there when we finish an album. For a start there's too many people in the control room . . . we play for months and do it, and then he leaves it to us.

ZZ: Do you wanna talk about any of the new songs?
KR: There's so many. I'm still trying to sort 'em out into tracks that are finished—there's a few that are mixed and done—then there's some which are good songs where the ideas are pretty much there but we need to recut 'em. Some have no lyrics yet, people humming away over the top of the track or the drums come in halfway through cos we started it when Charlie was in the bog, all those sort of things. There's some stuff I've totally forgotten about.

ZZ: You played on Ian MacLagen's album recently, didn't you?
KR: Yeah . . . I was on "Truly" and a recut of a song on Ronnie's first album ("Mystifies Me"). We did it at the end of the Barbarians tour.

ZZ: Another one—that Black Uhuru single.
KR: Yeah. "Shine Eye." That was those sessions I did with Sly and Robbie. It was just a backing track when I did it, then somebody said it'd come out with Black Uhuru singing on it.

That was one of the best things I did, to hang about in Jamaica after we'd done "Goat's Head Soup." I stayed there for nearly a year. I don't get down to Jamaica as much as I'd like to—every time I go down there I have a great time with this little band of Rastas I've played with for years. Just drums and chanting. They really kept me at it.

ZZ: Are you itching to get back on the road again?
KR: Yeah, I am a bit. I thought when we finished this last album that we'd get on the road now, but now I've sort of gotten over that and got used to the idea . . . I'm into finishing this other one, making it as good as we can, at the same time trying to set up some gigs, not waiting till we finish the album again before we think of what we're gonna do, but try and

work it so we've got something to do when we finish the album. I wanna get them on the road because, Mick and me have been playing one way or another—working on this album—but you forget we haven't played together with the other guys since we stopped cutting this time last year. It's a year since we even played together! So, get this one done as efficiently and quickly as possible (laughs) . . .

I know I wanna tour Europe. I can't see that until about March or April cos the weather screws up tours. In the winter you can't ever be sure of making a gig, not every one. There's a lot of places we ain't played for a long time. We want to play here but they just make it very difficult for us, y'know—taxes, there's a lot of red tape for us to play here. On top of that you don't get promoters and tour managers saying you gotta play England' cos you don't make any bread out of it. We don't expect to make any, but if they're not gonna make any bread they're not gonna push us to play England. We have to say, "look, we wanna play England, set it up." Otherwise it just doesn't appear on the list of things to do, which is dumb because there's no reason why we shouldn't play here more often.

ZZ: Yeah, cos I wondered how you still related to the kids here, the people who buy the records and all that.
KR: Well that's why I try and come back here as much as I can, just to see what's going on. Just soak it up and hand around, go and see bands . . .

ZZ: Do you talk much to the fans, geezers who come up to you? (IE: Is he really an untouchable 'cept for the jet set a la Rod Stewart, or—as I suspected anyway—did he still care what the kids thought, if they existed)
KR: Yeah. All different kinds, that's the whole thing innit? Half the time you find you're surrounded by middle-aged guys—"I saw you in the California Ballroom, Dunstable." You get surprising people coming up. Kids too. If I had longer time to spend I'd get into it a lot more.

ZZ: The Stones are often presented as a bit cut off.
KR: Remember who cut us off. It weren't us. We were kicked out. It was that or . . . they tried to put us in the can. They couldn't do that so they

decided to force us out economically, which they did. They just taxed the arse off us so we couldn't afford to keep the operation going unless we got out. Nobody's out through their own choice. I mean, we can live with it. By now, after travelling all these years, it doesn't really bother me where I am as long as I know I can come back occasionally. If we hadn't been kicked out I've no doubt we'd all still be here. It wasn't a matter of choice it was a matter of no choice. Get out. That was it. I mean, it's understandable—yeah the Stones are rich, tax exiles, blah, blah, blah, but it's only alright if you can live like that. Charlie came to live back in England, has for a year or two. If we hadn't been used to being on the road all the time I don't s'pose any of us would've wanted to go, wouldn't have gone. But we wouldn't have been able to keep the Stones together and stay in England, so it was a matter of having to get out. Now I've got used to it. No point in moaning, the only thing I wouldn't do is what they've tended to do over the last few years, bugger off to Los Angeles and live in that weird cut off climate out there. That Rod Stewart syndrome. I probably could've have got like that if they hadn't rubbed my nose in the shit so many times so that I never forgot the smell of it (laughs). In a way I don't really mind all the shit I've had to go through. At least it kept me in touch with reality when I could well have gone off the realms of . . . anywhere for a while! Eventually it got to a point where . . . if I was Joe Blow I probably could've stayed on dope forever as long as I could just sit in me little corner and have nothing to do but it had to reach that point in Canada where I thought, "I don't wanna be busted anymore, I don't wanna go through this shit anymore, knock it on the head," y' know.

(I'll just butt in 'ere. Before the interview, I made a mental note not to dive into the murky realms of Sunday paper "shocking Truth about Drug Fiend Keith" obsessions unless he brought this well-dredged skeleton up himself. So much has been written and speculated on the man's private life hobbies it would just seem predictable and brainless to try and prise more juice out of his weary and battered reputation. On the other hand, dope has been close to his heart for years. Now he's brought the subject up as the conversation gains momentum, so that's alright).

ZZ: You'll always be lumbered with the rock 'n' roll junkie chic number, won'tcha Keith?

(The man passes a hand over the thatch, which remains standing up in that position, lights another of my fags and the bourbon drawl creaks on.)
KR: Yeah . . . I ain't gonna get rid of that one easy am I? (laughs) Maybe if I keep my nose clean as long as I kept it dirty they'll forget about it.

ZZ: Do you still get hassles about it?
KR: No . . . no. S'funny. (leans forward and whacks table) Touch wood! It's like they've said, "oh we've had a go at him he's done his bit, we'll leave him alone, he's kept his end up" . . . which I certainly didn't do for them. I did it for the Stones and for myself, the kids, whatever . . .

ZZ: They pry into your private life, put all the dirt in lights . . . then say you're a bad influence on the kids.
KR: Right. Not only would you get done for what you got done for, you get done for setting a bad example. If they hadn't have come smashing through my front door no-one would've known what example I was setting! They made it public, not me. I could understand it if I'd gone round saying, "oh yeah have a needle and a spoon, go off and have a good time, that's what it's all about." But I wasn't about to go round advertising it, they advertised it, then I had to pay for it. But fuck it, it happens to lots of people.

I don't know how much the powers that be all work together or communicate with each other but it was like, how many more times would they have done me without it looking really like a bit of, "let's pick on him," y'know? I was an easy target. They knew I was on the stuff. They could've come round every day! That's why I eventually had to say "no more." I don't wanna see 'em anymore. I was seeing more of cops and lawyers than I was of anybody else. To my mind in the business of crime there's two people involved and that's the criminal and the cops. It's in both their interests to keep crime a business, otherwise they're both out of a job. So they're gonna look for it, they ain't gonna wait for it to 'appen.

ZZ: I just read Tony Sanchez' book . . .
KR: Ohh . . . Grimm's fairy stories, yeah! Unbelievable, that. When it got to the blood change bit I thought, "oh, here we go!" Marvellous. "Then he sprouted wings."

(The book, "Up And Down with the Rolling Stones"—so far published just in the States—consists of the "memoirs" of Keith's old bodyguard—right-handman Spanish Tony, who really lays on the heavy Dope exploits. Keith emerges as a hard, selfish doper who changes his blood more often than his socks. The gutter press has already serialised bits, Tone makes a packet. Keith dismisses it with a grin and a shrug. What's the point getting steamed up, launching injunctions and losing sleep. More "past acquaintances" have made more money out of the Stones than anyone else.)

KR: It wasn't him who wrote it, just some hack from Fleet Street. I'm the nasty, dirty, yellow schnide—oh nice, Tony, thanks, you're my friend! Actually it's quite clever. The actual incidents all happened, but then halfway through each chapter the description takes off into fantasy. This guy says Mick and I buried Brian, we made sure that nobody would ever see him again . . . the guy's gotta make an angle or how ye gonna sell the book? The Fleet Street hack thinks in terms of headlines. Spanish Tony had been with us for a long time, and a lot of the incidents in broad outline happened, but some of the details . . . I just gave up on the blood change! It's surprising the number of people believe all that. No doubt some people do it.

That one came about like this: I'd been in a clinic in Switzerland. Spanish Tony came to help us move into a house—I was still in the clinic. Tony: "What did they do to you up there?" Since I could hardly remember anyway and I'd only been in there about a week—I'd just crashed out virtually, went around puking in the ashtrays, ripping down the furniture and fittings for a couple of days and then I'd sort of got better, as usual. So I couldn't explain all this to Tony so I said, "ohh, they took all my blood out and gave me some fresh blood, all cleaned up." And slowly over the years that one sentence has become one huge . . . "oh the blood-change man," y'know? It's funny, one remark because you can't be bothered to explain and before you know it that's what you are. They probably wouldn't have sold any books without that.

ZZ: *What about Brian though? (In the book the hapless original Stones guitarist who died mysteriously in a swimming pool in 1969 is depicted as a drugged shell beaten into the ground by police oppression and paranoia fostered by heartless colleagues stealing his thunder. No-one will ever know the true circumstances of his death but it remains one of rock's biggest tragedies—and most ironic, seeing as he was on the way back up with a new band and healthier outlook.)*

KR: He was getting in a real state towards the end. That was the main reason he eventually left the band. He was just no longer in touch with anything. Although he was real strong in lots of ways, he just found his weakness that night, whatever happened. I still take all the stories from that night with a pinch of salt. I've no doubt it's the same with anybody when those things happen. There's a crowd of people, then suddenly there's nobody there. Instead of trying to help the guy, they think of their own skins and run. It's the same as what happened to Gram Parsons— someone gave him a turn-on, he passed out and they all got chicken and ran without even calling the ambulance or anything.

ZZ: Anyway from the morbid subjects . . .

KR: Industrial accidents . . . I dunno, either. In my own head I think about it and reach the same conclusion as last time, or I start to think about it again and get another idea on it. If you're not actually there when those things go down you can never say . . . I don't know what really went on that night at Brian's place. I know there was a lot of people there and suddenly there wasn't and that's about it. Yeah off that subject, right?

ZZ: Okay. Back to the album. Do you think people didn't bother to listen to "Emotional Rescue" properly before slagging it away?

KR: I dunno. I remember "Exile on Main Street" being slagged all over the place when it came out and then the SAME guys six years later holding it up and saying, "oh this new album's not as good as 'EXILE ON MAIN STREET'," I read about two or three reviews when they come out and that's it.

It's a number one record, and it sold well. We've done what we intended to do—put out a record; after all, it's popular music. Unpopular music is about the worst thing you can make. I'd rather it be popular. So I'd rather use that criteria than two or three writers slagging it off.

ZZ: . . . They say the Stones don't stand up to the groups around today (you know who).

KR: (With a tinge of cold irritation) Well that's the bands they like. A lot of the bands they like don't mean fuckall anywhere to anybody. Whether they might in the future, I ain't slagging the bands. It all depends where you live. No doubt if we'd all stayed in England we'd be playing and doing things differently than the fact that we had to move out . . . you start picking up music from wherever you start to live or where you start to move around, y'know. A lot of it didn't turn out to be that different, whether I was in England or not. We've been playing reggae between ourselves and into reggae for over ten years, just about since it really started to emerge as its own form, So that kept us in touch with a lot of what's happening in England just by coincidence in a way. We just happened to be in Jamaica. And at that time soul music had taken a dive cos Disco had taken over. That was about the only black music we could find that was still fresh. They gave us something we used to get out of American black music. So it was just a natural substitute, in a way. At the same time a progression. But when we started listening to reggae *nobody* wanted to know, 'specially rock 'n' roll musicians—they couldn't understand it cos the beat's turned round. Now a lot of kids have grown up with it, on the street, there's a lot of Jamaicans here and they've brought their music with 'em. Now it's mixing up and you've got black guys coming out and playing supercharged rock. That's what's interesting, that's what keeps music going. If it just stayed the same as the three or four reviewers people read wanted it to stay, or just because it isn't like their pet favourite of the moment . . . people say the public's fickle but critics are ten times more fickle than the public!

ZZ: "Some Girls" got a favourable reception compared to "Emotional Rescue."

KR: Yeah, "Some Girls" . . . just because of the time it came out, etc etc, and the circumstances—very favourable reaction there, but you know that the next one's gonna get slagged, "oh they're just marking time again." But we've just done what we've always done, we'll go in and make a record. We'll go in and make it as good as we can in the period of time that we've got to make it in—which is a long time sometimes, but the bigger a band gets and the bigger its organisation gets, the longer everything takes. This is one thing I'm always fighting against, saying "it shouldn't be like that," but it's just a fact of life. The more people involved, the bigger the size of the record company, the bigger the importance . . . it just takes longer. I mean we made the first one in ten days, and several of the others too. But now it's A Rolling Stones Album and you feel you've gotta work and work on it, polish it up . . . and eventually you give in to that pressure a lot of the time, then afterwards you wish you'd just slammed it out like this rough mix on a cassette. I always try and push it. F'rinstance "Dance" on "Emotional Rescue," I wanted to keep instrumental. The track's dynamite by itself. Putting the vocal on it I felt—and I still feel in a way cos I've got the instrumental track at home—just detracted enough from the track for nobody to really listen to the vocals either. To me it was a kind of compromise. I'd have much rather kept the track as it was.

It became a compromise - do the vocals again but rewrite it. You win some, you give a little, you take a little, and I wanted "All about You" on there. But if I wanna listen to "Dance" I play the cassette of the track!

(I'm steadily building up this picture of the Stones at Work. Keith with his bits bartering with Jagger over what goes on "well if I can 'ave "All about You" and you take those ridiculous vocals off "Dance" you can keep "Emotional Rescue" AND "Send It to Me" on the album, 'ow's about that, Mick?" There's the nagging irritation that "Emotional Rescue" would've been a KILLER if Keith'd had his way more.)

KR: But it's always a compromise, because it's for a specific reason. You're saying this is it, but we all know there's lot of stuff left on the floor which a lot of people like as well. The trouble is you just can't please everybody with one album, it's not possible. Everybody wants to hear their idea of what the Stones is. There's the old-timers who remember from the year dot, then you've got the ones who believe we popped out of the ground with "Satisfaction," then there's the lot who joined us with "Beggars Banquet," the "Brown Sugar" lot. There's people who didn't get into us till the 70s. Everybody's got their own idea of what the Stones are about, which I suppose gets more and more confusing the longer you exist.

ZZ: *It gets impossible to live up to all that.*

KR: Well it gets impossible if you *try* and live up to it. We just do what we do and hope they like it. I mean usually you find more and more that people come up with interesting ideas on an album a year later. Me too. It'll take that long to get a little perspective on the last album. I'm too close to it right now. I've only just healed up from the last sessions! (laughs). Beat me own record—nine days on a stretch! Once you get in the Studio it doesn't really matter. It's timeless, like hibernation (giggle)! One tape op drops, you wake another one up!

ZZ: *How dya keep awake then?*
KR: I dunno, I can only do it when I'm working really. I've got a cycle of it by now, I get up and I'll be up for two or three days, but when you're working—I mean, Ronnie and I, when we were doing the '75 tour in the States at Madison Square Gardens—six nights in a row—we didn't sleep from the first gig till the end of the sixth one. I guess it was because we were stuck in the same place suddenly—same hotel, same theatre—and you feel like you're a record that's just got stuck! You don't think of sleeping. I don't remember the last three gigs. We'd just go off somewhere and turn up at the Garden for the next gig. God knows what we did, we just wandered about! We were well out of it I know that! It gets down to the point where you go round and bug people—you don't just go and visit someone, it's "let's find someone we really don't like and go round and bug 'em!" It's just so rare we find ourselves at the same place for a week in a tour. It's like a summer season at Great Yarmouth pier. (Keith goes on to bemoan the lack of decent venues in Britain, 'specially London. Obviously Hammersmith's a bit small and he don't wanna do the monstrous make-shift Earls Court. "London's eleven million people, you'd think they could rake up enough for a decent stadium, five thousand seater or something." He mentions the buzz he got when the Stones did some three thousand seaters in the States. "Kept us on our toes. It's a totally different way of playing."

"Put an ad in—anybody wanna bug a lotus-shaped stage. That's as far as I want to take *that* one!"

He's still with Anita Pallenburg "she's in good spirits nowadays, she's been through a lot of shit too." Son Marlon's at school—"he's too fuckin' bright, I'm trying to retard him"—and the Richards are on the move again cos their lease has run out.

ZZ: Thought any more about doing a solo album? What's happened to all these tracks you laid down in Canada?
KR: People always ask me cos they know I did those tracks. I mean I do 'em because the opportunities there in the studio. For some reason nobody else has turned up . . . at the time I do them I just do 'em. I'm still in the same state of mind as always, like Mick. I'm not interested in splitting meself up to the point where I'm going "I'm going to keep this for me, that's a nice song I won't give it to the Stones": put yourself in that position it's stupid. One thing at a time—if I'm in the Stones I'm in the Stones and I make Stones records. If I'm not in the Stones, I'll think about doing my own record. I don't wanna split my loyalties.

ZZ; What about your solo single, "Run—Rudolph Run"?
KR: Oh yeah. I put that out, I just wanted to put out a Christmas record, why not? I had it around for a while—stick it out. And the other side "Harder They Come" is an even bigger jumble. It was like a quick snatch of tape we'd done between two other songs—did it during a break. But there's nothing on the actual record that was on the tape. Eventually we overdubbed it and wiped everything that was on there off. There's nothing left of the original tape. Ronnie ended up doing most of the drums on it. There's a couple of mistakes in it, I don't care. Some of the records I like best have got mistakes all over 'em. So we put it on the "B" side of "Rudolph."

ZZ: You've been involved with Ron Wood's solo projects.
KR: Yeah, he doesn't have the pressure like me 'n' Mick of having to write for the Stones. I mean, if he's got a good song we do it, some of his ideas and riffs and stuff we have used, that's fine, the pressure isn't on him to come up with stuff for the Stones and at the same time I know he enjoyed doing the first one and I enjoyed doing it with him ("I've Got My Own Album to Do"), but after that it's really been, "you owe the record company an album." And that's what he's still doing. He's doing it cos he's got

to now, not cos he wants to. It's ultimately his own fault in a way, he let himself get in that position, but Ronnie's not the sort of bloke to under-stand what they're all doing behind the scenes until they've got him tied up in a nice neat parcel and he's got to cough up with the songs and an album, which he'll enjoy doing while he's doing it but it's not something he would've done unless he'd had to do it. There's nothing worse than making an album just to fulfill a contract. That's like work! You stop play-ing and start working. I mean, we call it work but to meself, working . . . that's something I've tried to avoid all my life! (laughs) I've always tried to avoid feeling like I'm working anyway.

ZZ: You must be quite pleased how it turned out. There's lot of kids start playing the guitar for fun.
KR: Yeah right, that's what I thought when we had two gigs a week—oh great! No more schlepping around this artwork trying to get a job in an advertising agency and I chucked it. "I'm making a tenner a week, en 'I ? I'm alright! As long as I don't break strings or a valve goes in the ampli-fier I'll come out with a fiver at the end of the week. Be alright!" So it was always like that, they just added more zeroes on the end as it went on, but as far as I'm concerned it's the same attitude since we got our first gig— "fine, great, wow, I'm doing what I really wanna do, and they're paying me to do it!"

ZZ: What's your favourite thing that you've done? Is there any one thing you can pick out?
KR: Ohh wow . . . umm . . . that was easy to answer years ago when there wasn't so much to choose from or remember! Fairly broadly speaking, without picking out particular songs or anything, going backwards as albums go. I was very happy with the last one. I like it, and "Some Girls." More and more now I've been listening to "Black and Blue." Quite like some of that, considering especially that I know the ins 'n' outs of how it was made—that album was put together while auditioning guitar players, trying to find a new guy (to replace Mick Taylor), It's interesting for me to listen to "Black and Blue" because there's a different guitar player on virtually every track, Wayne Perkins, Harvey Mandel, other people came

round and played with us—even Jeff Beck, who I get on with now but at that time we were sort of glowering over the guitars.

ZZ: Another classic from 'round then was "Time Waits for No One" (more under-rated Stones emotion—this time on the passing of time—they ain't just a rock 'n' roll boogie squad, y'know. Mick Taylor's solo is a classic.)
KR: That was the last thing Mick Taylor did with us. Why don't Mick Taylor kick himself in the arse and realise what he is? He's a fuckin' great guitar player. If he'd stop pissing about trying to be a songwriter, a producer, a bandleader. At the time it was probably the right thing for him to do (leave the group), for him and us. But he hasn't done a thing since he left which he couldn't have done with us. It was his decision to leave. If he'd decided to stay he could still be with us now probably. What's he come up with? One album and a couple of gigs with Jack Bruce.

ZZ: His album was pure crap.
KR: That's what I mean. If only he'd realise what he is, a damn good guitar player. He should find somebody to play with. He's a bit lazy and while he's still got our royalties coming in he'll just indulge himself—produce, write, be the drummer . . . he's not a guy to make quick decisions and if you produce a record you've gotta be able to say even if you're wrong, "rub that out." That's why albums take so long these days. That's the other side of recording—the technology. Every time you do four more tracks you put another two months on the album. When we started if the record didn't sound right at the playback, tough shit because that was it! There was nothing else you could do!

ZZ: When you play live that's it too.
KR: Yeah, you've still gotta be able to do it, but it's the other way round. You write the song and record it then work out a way of doing it live. That's not the natural way to do it is play it live until you've got it honed down real good and THEN record it. But then nobody wants to hear you play material they don't know. That's the other thing with being in a band like the Stones—you've always got 'em down the front going "Satisfaction!," "Play with Fire"! Everybody's got their old favourites, they don't

wanna hear the new stuff—until it's out on the record and they've bought it and got it at home, then they wanna hear it. Wanna shot of this?

Keith offers his bottle, realises what he just said and adds into my recorder, "when I say shot of this, it's a drink!" We take a break to find a light switch.

ZZ: How's your guitar style going—still pretty much sticking to rhythm?
KR: Me 'n' Ronnie should play more together, but finishing the record has put the mockers on it recently. I enjoy playing with Ronnie a lot because . . . I think the main thing about making records is to produce a sound. I've never been that interested in being a guitar-player as such on my own, by myself. Sometimes I surprise meself, sometimes I disappoint myself. I'm more interested in what sound you can produce. This is why I've never really been interested in bands with only one guitar player, unless they've got something else going. Bass, drums 'n' guitar just ain't enough for me, there ain't enough to make a sound. Ronnie knows that and we can get into that a lot, especially if we play a lot together. But we're gonna have to do a bit of swotting up cos we ain't played lately!

ZZ: He mainly takes the lead lines, doesn't he?
KR: A lot of the time. Mainly, I guess, cos if I'd written the song then I'll get into knocking out the chords with Charlie so everyone can learn it, so by the time we've got it together the roles are pretty much fixed cos of that. Usually there's a lot more than two guitars on any of our records. I over-dub, and usually you can't distinguish the overdub, you might only hear it as distinctive sound once or twice in the record—I'll just mesh it in with the other guitars and pull it out here and there. We're more interested in the sound—that's being made rather than who's playing what.

ZZ: Still got that guitar with the daggers and devils on it?
KR: That went up in flames. We had a fire in my house. Ronnie had that made for me, I used to use it a lot. It was a custom job, Zematis. There was a fire—didn't even get me trousers on, just jumped out the window! There were all these neighbours worried about the flames catching their houses. I was standing there—"wadya want me to do, pee on it? Forget it!"

Keith leafs through a recent *Zigzag* and notices the embarrassing American Heroin Scene overview, which I'd tried to keep out cos I thought it cheap, superficial and irresponsible (I was over-ruled). The first line went, "Heroin is not chic" and a quote about Stones drug references in songs is blown up as a headline. As Keith scans this gutter-scraping I cringe and foresee an abrupt termination of our conversation. He reads, grim and tight-lipped. Looks up . . .

KR: There's no way of writing about anything like that. It doesn't matter which way you angle it or state your case. Somebody's going to get turned on by it. Saying it's "not chic," that means it's chic. If you said it was chic . . . there's no way of writing about it because it's such an emotional and sensitive subject. The main thing is, why, especially in this business, do people go on to it in the first place? What are the pressures? Is it the one guy above you that you dig the way he plays. Charlie Parker has done more to turn lots of horn-players into junkies just because it happened to be known. If people had left him alone and nobody had known he was a junkie, maybe it would've been better. Why go searching out making sensational stories when you know that, just because the cops bust somebody if they're popular musicians or a superstar, there's gonna be somebody, no matter what that guy's going through himself, who's going to try and emulate it in some way? There's no right way of writing about heroin. There's plenty of wrong ways and it's difficult to know. Ever since I kicked it and cleaned up I've been bombarded with requests and offers to make a statement about this, or address judges—I've been asked to do lectures for judges! What would I say in front of 800 judges? The chance I've been waiting for—FUCK YOU! What else am I gonna say to them about dope? I'd just be embroiling myself and keeping myself in the same bag and attaching myself to the same thing that I'm trying to get rid of. Probably the only thing that might have any effect is, once everybody knows you're a junky then yeah, you are an example. They've made you one, whether you wanna be or not. So the only example I can be now is to say, yeah, I've done it for longer than most people and luckily came out the other end and I'm still here and I'm alright. Even if you're into it already and you need to kick it, at least you know, because I'm still 'ere. If you want to you can kick it and the sooner the better, darlin'. If there's one thing I can talk about more than Music and guitars, I can talk about dope (laughs). It's like guns. There's nothing wrong with the gun, it's the people who're on the trigger. Guns are an inanimate object, a Heroin needle's an inanimate object. It's what's done with it that's important. I think of all these people doing it and not even knowing what they're doing. That to me is the dumbest thing. At least by the time I got on it I knew as much as you can know. The one thing I've realised more than anything since I kicked it is that the criteria you use when you're on it is so distorted from what you'd use normally. I know the angle—waiting for the man, sitting in some goddam basement waiting for some creep to come, with four other guys snivelling, puking and retching around, and you're waiting for something to happen, and it's already been 24 hours and you're going into the worst. How does it feel, baby? You don't feel great. If I was Joe Blow maybe I'd still be on it, I dunno. I wouldn't take any notice of what I was saying if I was listening to it or anybody else, cos when you're on it you don't. The only thing I can say is, if you want to, it's no big deal to kick it. Everybody wants to make like, "oh, I've been to Hell and back." You've only been half-way, baby. Nobody's been there and back. Anyway, here I am. Ten years I did it and then I stopped and I'm still 'ere. I've still got two legs, two arms luckily and a bit of a head left, and that's about it. If examples count at all that's the only statement I can make: I'm still here.

In America it's even worse cos you have doctors coming on TV, discussions about the drug problem. These doctors—the more patients they get on methadone (heroin substitute), the bigger federal grant they get, so it's in their interest. They tell people who've been on it a few months, a year, "your body can never do without heroin, you'll need methadone forever." Bullshit. You can kick it in three fucking days. That's as long as it stays in ya. After that it's up to you. I might oversimplify it in saying that, but that's the way it's always hit me. It's a physical thing for me in almost every way. If I can kick those three days . . .

The other big problem is not cleaning them up, just sending 'em back. The same with me. The times I cleaned up and went back to exactly the same scene I was in before. What else you gonna do? You've been doing it for years. Everybody you know's doing it, you're kind of locked in. Unless you can break out of that circle afterwards—that's the next step.

You're back in that same room as five years before when you were on it and they're still calling you up, some people are coming around. It's a total drug, like total war. It takes over your whole life, every aspect of it eventually.

I used to clean up to do a tour, cos I just didn't want to be on the road and have to be hassled. But physically having to readjust when a tour just stops. (snaps fingers.) "*Now* what do I do?" I'm physically readjusting to then going home and living a quiet family life for two months. That'd do me in. Boredom, I'd go back on it. But if I had to work I'd clean up. But what a hassle! But when you're on it you'll go through any hassle to get it. "First get me the dope then I'll do what I have to do."

ZZ: I bet you had a never-ending stream of fawners who gave you stuff so they could boast they supplied Keith Richard.

KR: Oh sure. It was "great to see you man, I need it and you got it." You've got that to deal with as well, people stuffing it at ya. There's no way I could explain that in Aylesbury court. The things that are given to us. But I knew there was no point in trying to explain it to straight jury and a judge, even to my own lawyer. All the time, they think they're doing you a favour and probably at the time I thought so too. Some kid sends me an envelope with a quarter of an ounce of smack in it, y'know, "have a good time, Keith, thumbs up, yeah right, whaay." If you're on it you'll go "yeah right, whaay" back, cos you need it and you're not gonna say no.

But really nobody's doing anybody a favour.

Once I cleaned up and viewed it all from a bit of perspective . . . dealers would still be coming up to me. I'd dig just watching their faces. One thing that got me over that second period of cleaning up the environment was seeing these dealers' faces when they realised there was no sale! (laughs) It was a perverse way of going about it but it got me through the period.

The morbid mood lifts again as the talk drifts back, this time to the earliest days of the Stones. Keith's highly amused when I tell him that the Bricklayers' Arms, the pub off Wardour Street where the Stones rehearsed for their earliest gigs, is now a violin shop, and ("must've had some influence somewhere") retaliates with a tale about original pianist Ian Stewart forgetting the breaks cos he was eying the Soho strippers out the window. The laminated elbow-grasping Mike Yarwood doing his "Cor I could shaft that!" impersonation of Stewart is a far cry from the Devil's right-hand man of popular repute.

Keith described how he and Jagger initially developed their prolific songwriting partnership. I'd never heard this one before . . .

"I can thank Andrew Oldham (their first manager) for many things, but more than anything thank him for forcing me to sit down and write these horrendous songs, cos when you start it's always the worst. We'd farm them off to somebody else cos we didn't wanna know. Gene Pitney, Marianne Faithfull? Sure, have this one. You've gotta get all that shit outta your system before you can really start writing. At the time you write 'em you're even amazed you can write that. 'I'm just the guitar-player.' Hats off to Andrew for that one just for making me find out I could do it."

ZZ: Your first composition on record was "Tell Me," right?
KR: Yeah, and that was a demo. Andrew stuck it on the album because we needed another track. It was cut as a demo and Andrew was gonna try and flog it off to somebody. But we bunged it on. In America it was the first thing we did that got pulled out. Then we realised about songwriting. Apart from playing, that's the other thing I enjoy doing more than anything, trying to hammer out a new song.

Keith had to go so I trotted off, well pleased. He's a good geezer and he still cares. Who'll shoot KR? Not me.

7 |

TATTOO ME

GIL MARKLE | 1981

In July 1981, Keith Richards made a quick decision to locate the Rolling Stones' rehearsals for their *Tattoo You* tour at a sprawling, picturesque complex of recording studios located deep in the countryside of Massachusetts called Long View Farm. Studio owner Gil Markle made copious notes about Richards's inspection visit and the subsequent six-week stay of the Stones at the facility, eventually collating these into the book-length Internet monograph *Tattoo Me*. This entertaining cyber-volume has remained unpublished, save for the excerpts that follow here. Also unissued, incidentally, is the lengthy compilation of classic songs, some dating from the 1930s, that Markle found himself engineering for Richards who accompanied himself on piano. This widely bootlegged collection has come to be regarded as the definitive statement of the "solo" Richards.

"This is Cessna 75 X, intercom to base. 75 X, to base.

Tell Gil we have Keith plus four. Alan Dunn and wife, Jane Rose, and some knockout named Patti.

We're twenty miles out. Will call back over the Outer Marker.

Tell Gil to get the Cadillac cooling. We've got his man."

That was pilot Bob Adams. I switched off the scanner, grabbed my leather briefcase, and began the procedures for turning off the lights at our company headquarters at the Worcester Airport. Convenient, having your offices at the Airport, particularly if you have a twin-engine airplane. Long View shares its office space with the large student travel company

I started as a graduate student at Yale, and to which I have continued to devote myself over the years.

One bank of lights went out after another. Mailroom, sales cubicles, computer room, overseas offices, travel agency, financial offices, acceptance division, finally Gil's office. I scooped up my gin & tonic, locked the stainless steel double doors, and lurched out into the warm summer night, toward the car, the arrival gate, and my night's work.

It had been a long day—the day of the Keith Richards creeping delay.

No, Keith could not possibly make it at two. He had a dentist's appointment at two. Keith was late for his dentist's appointment. No, Keith did not leave for the airport directly from the dentist's; he had to visit a friend first, on the way out of the city. What friend, or for what purpose, unknown. It was now suppertime. Keith was still at the friend's house, expecting to leave soon for Teterboro, but hadn't left yet. Keith finally leaves for Teterboro, it's thought. No one knows for sure. Gil calls Teterboro; no Keith, although the plane's there and waiting. Gil calls Teterboro a half-hour later; still no Keith. Gil calls Teterboro a half-hour later still; now 8:30 PM, or thereabouts.

"Charlotte. I'm glad it's you this time. It's Gil Markle. Listen, I've got some high-level clients meeting 75 X-Ray, any minute now. I'm calling to see if anybody's showed up yet."

"Who this time, Gil?"

"Never mind, Charlotte, it doesn't matter. Should be a group of four or five, some English. Seen anybody like that, Charlotte? Charlotte? You there, Charlotte?"

I heard a loud noise, as though Charlotte had dropped the receiver onto the floor. Commotion. Charlotte's voice, high pitched and squeaking.

"Gil," she gasped into the phone. "You'll never guess who just walked in the door. Je-sus . . ."

"It's not Keith Richards by any chance, is it Charlotte?"

"Gil," she said with determination, "I hate you."

That's when I first knew we had our man. Also, that's when I first knew, or felt, that my meditation was projecting itself out into the world in conformity with the manifest wishes of others, and hence the Grand Design; I mean, that the Rolling Stones were coming to Long View Farm.

I looked at the clock, switched on the aircraft scanner, and went down to the bar for a gin & tonic.

I had now only another hour or so to wait.

Keith ambled out of the airplane, legs stiff from the 45 minute trip from Teterboro. He smiled. Keith looked like warm, friendly leather. Soft eyes.

"I'm Gil Markle, Keith. Welcome here."

"Hey, yeah. Nice, man. Nice trip."

"And I'm Alan Dunn, Gil. Sorry for the delay, but here we are."

I was then introduced to Jane Rose, who was talking to Keith and looking at him while shaking my hand, to Alan's comely wife Maureen, and to a smiling Patti Hansen, who looked me right in the eyes.

"Let's go," I said. "Black car, over there."

"We all going in one car?" Keith asked.

"Yes," I said. "We'll all fit." I made a mental note to investigate the purchase of a second black Cadillac. (Except they didn't build big ones anymore.) We squeezed into the car. Keith, Patti, and Jane Rose in the back seat; Alan Dunn and his wife up front; me driving.

"Car got a radio?" Keith shouted up.

I flipped to WAAF, The Police; then to WBCN, an old J. Geils cut; then to some Hartford station, Jerry Lee Lewis.

"Yeah," Keith erupted. "Yeah."

I turned up the volume, and by the end of the tune, which was "Personality," we were gliding up Stoddard Road, past the Long View pond and rowboat, and up the long gravel drive. The Farmhouse glistened white, and the enormous barn glowed cherry red under a dark but very starry summer's night sky. There was a new moon. It was silent, except for the crickets.

"Welcome to Long View, Keith," I said.

"Yeah," Keith replied. "Nice place."

We were scarcely inside the house, drinks ordered up but not yet in hand, when Alan Dunn motioned to me and took me aside, behind the fireplace. "Look," he said, "this has got to be quick tonight. I've got to be back in the city for a day's work tomorrow. So does Jane Rose. Keith's got to be in Rome before the weekend, and he's nowhere near ready to go. Just got evicted from his apartment, and there're a lot of loose ends to tie up. So give him a quick tour, and let's take a look at your plans for the loft. Don't get your hopes up. There's just not time for us to do much tonight."

"Here's your wine, Alan," I said. "And here's a screwdriver for Keith. Where'd he go?"

"Into the control room, I think. With Patti. Let's meet up in the loft in ten minutes, and you better call your pilots and tell them to be ready to depart Worcester for Teterboro at eleven, at the latest. Sorry it's got to be so rushed, but this was your idea, not mine."

"Ten minutes, Alan, in the loft."

It took us twenty minutes to get up there, not ten. Keith was in no hurry, and neither was I, if you want to know the truth. We hung out in the control room for a while, and I explained to him how we have tie lines between the two studios, and how we sometimes record over across the way, in the barn, but mix here in Control Room A. We then took a look at the bedrooms upstairs, the balcony overlooking our antique Steinway, and our collection of records.

"You keep all your fifties in one place, too," he remarked with apparent relief. "Easier that way, isn't it? That cassette deck work?"

"Sure does, Keith. What you got there?"

"Bunch of stuff all mixed up. Starts with some Buddy Holly, I think."

Keith slammed the cassette into the cassette deck, which hangs at eye level just as you enter the kitchen, and hit the "go" button.

"Select tape two on the pre-amp," I shouted over to him, which he did.

On came Buddy Holly, as expected. Keith turned it up, loud, very loud, until it began to distort the JBLs hanging overhead, then down just a notch. Maximum undistorted volume, that's called. He extended his glass to me, which now had only a bit of yellow left in it, way down at the bottom of the glass. He needed a refill.

"Good idea," I said. "Then let's go across the way and I'll show you what we have in mind for the stage."

"Yeah," Keith said. "Let's go over to the barn. Got to find Patti, though. Hold on a minute."

Patti materialized, and we headed out, through the library, under the moosehead, past the fish tank, and out onto the driveway.

"Look down there, Keith," I said. "Those lights down there are Stanley's, and he's our nearest neighbor. Farmer."

"Hope he likes rock 'n' roll," Keith laughed.

"He better by now," I said. "He's been hearing it from us for almost eight years now. Up these stairs here, and straight ahead."

Alan Dunn and Jane Rose were waiting for us in the loft, and had already been briefed by Geoff Myers, who was talking in an animated fashion, and moving his arms in wide arcs. He was explaining how deep the stage was going to be, and how strong. Keith listened for a moment, then walked over to one of the massive support beams, and kicked it. He looked up, whistled softly through his teeth, and spun around slowly, on his heel.

"Yeah," he said. "What's down there?"

"Come on, I'll show you," and I scrambled down the rickety ladder into what we now call the Keith Richards bedroom suite. Keith followed, with Jane Rose telling him to be careful.

"We don't really know how strong that thing is, now, do we? Gil, are you sure you need Keith down there? Why don't you just leave Keith up here and you can talk to us from down there. Keith, are you all right? Keith!"

"Figured we'd do a bedroom and living area down here," I said. "Right beside the chimney here. A place for people to hang out during the rehearsals, but still be out of the way. Look up there. The stage will be on the level of those transverse beams. You'll be able to see the whole thing from down here. We'll build staircases, fix it up nice. Cassette deck will be over there; speakers hanging so, on either side of the chimney. Should sound good down here."

Keith looked up at the chimney, then back at me. I saw a gleam in his eye. We had this one.

Keith and I made our way back up the ladder, Keith first, much to Jane Rose's pleasure and relief. Geoff Myers was jumping up and down on the plank floor, trying to make it move.

"See? And this is just one layer of two-inch pine on top of two-by-eights. Nothing compared to the strength of the stage, which will have three layers: beams of hemlock, pine sub-flooring, and oak finish. You could drive a truck up there and the floor wouldn't give a bit."

And that's all Keith needed to hear. He walked up to Geoff, and gave him a friendly slap on the lapel with the back of his hand.

"It won't bounce, right?"

"No bounce, Keith."

"We're coming, then. What a place I found!"

"We're what?" Alan interrupted.

"We're coming to this man's barn. Where's Mick now?"

"India, Keith."

"Let's go ring him. What a place I found!"

"How's your screwdriver, Keith?" I asked. It was plainly down to its ice cubes, and needed refreshing.

He looked at me, and at my screwdriver, which was still quite yellow, and full of Stoli.

I poured my glass into his; he laughed, and we walked back across the driveway to the Farmhouse. Keith and I were getting on just fine.

"Oh, Keith! Keith!" Jane Rose tends to shriek a bit when she talks. Her job is to take care of Mick Jagger and Keith Richards, and she's very protective of them.

"Oh, I knew I'd find you in here, in this ice-cold control room, talking to Greg and listening to records."

Keith hit the "mute" button on the console, lowering the volume level in the room.

"Gil's his name," he said.

"Gil, then. Listen, Keith-eee, we simply must begin to think about getting on our way. Greg, here—Gil, I mean—has those two pilots waiting inside that gorgeous airplane, and we simply can't keep them waiting, can we? You know what you have to do for tomorrow. There's the dentist again, and there's the Consulate, and there's Renaldo, in Rome, and we're way up here in goodness-knows-where. And I know Patti must get back to the city, too, mustn't you, dear, and I know . . ."

"We're not going anywhere," Keith said, returning the level of the studio monitors to full, undistorted blast.

"We're not going anywhere," he said again, I think, judging from the way his lips moved.

I smiled, having only moments ago taken Keith behind the moose head in the library with our two full glasses of Stoli and orange juice. "You don't have to go anywhere tonight, Keith," I had said. "It just starts to get fun here after supper. You can hang out, listen to some records, fool around, anything you want. The place is yours."

"Yeah," he muttered through a smile. "I don't have to go anywhere, do I?"

"No, Keith," I said, "you don't."

And he didn't go anywhere. Jane brought the word back outside to Alan, who was tired and just as happy to stay, and the pilots were released from any duty within Gil's gorgeous airplane. Keith stayed, and stayed largely inside the control room, playing and listening to music, for the better part of three days.

"Get Jane up," he said at one point. It's always dark in the control room, particularly when the black velvet curtains are pulled, and so it's difficult to tell what time it is, or whether it's night or day. I think it was about 5 AM. We had just gone through a half a dozen versions of Merle Haggard's "Sing Me Back Home," Keith singing and accompanying himself on the piano.

"Tell her to get Woody on the phone, and Bobby Keys, too."

"Keith," I asked, "do you know what time it is? I don't."

"Doesn't matter. I never get a chance to do this. You don't understand. I suppose you think it's all fun being me. Listen, I never get a chance to sing by myself like this—play the piano—without some bastard weirding out and asking me why I wasn't playing the guitar, and looking mean. People have their ideas about me. I bet you didn't think I could play the piano, did you? Or sing classics from the thirties. Well, I can, and I want to talk to Woody. He'll love it here. Where's Jane?"

"Upstairs, Keith, in the Crow."

"I'll go, Keith," volunteered Patti Hansen, and she slithered out the door and up the staircase to the bedroom we call the Crow. Muffled female voices indicated that Jane had not been sleeping all that soundly, if at all, and that she had some reservations about calling Woody and Bobby Keys.

"I know what you mean, Keith," I continued down below. "It's not all that great when you get what you want. Me, I've got a lot of things happening, but also a lot of screwed up relationships, like with my girlfriend, who's the mother of my kids."

"Me, too," Keith said, slapping his vest pocket and looking about for something he had obviously misplaced. "I did the same thing. Her name's Anita. Kid's Marlon."

"Here's what you're looking for," I said. "Use the razor in the editing block."

"People think I get my way a lot more than I do," Keith continued. "You don't know what it's like dealing with the people I have to deal with. If it wasn't for the music, I wouldn't be doing it."

Sniff!

"Let's do 'Dream' next, what d'ya think?"

"Let's do it, Keith. Gimme a minute, though. I want to put some two-inch tape on the big machine for this one. Something I want to check on the machine first, too."

"No hurry, man. No . . . hurry." Keith stretched out the "no's" until they wouldn't stretch any more, and addressed the mirror once again.

Sniff!

Patti Hansen leaned her full weight on the heavy studio door, opening it a crack and looking in on Keith and me.

"Look at the two of you. I mean, I can't leave the room for a minute. I need to talk to you, Gil. Come here, will you?"

"What's up, Patti?" I asked, a bit blinded once outside the door by the early morning light. "What's up?"

"You've got to invent some excuse, Jane says. He may never leave here if you don't. You don't know Keith. He likes it here, too much maybe. But he's got to be in Rome before next Monday to get his visa fixed. Jane's worried. Can't you say something about the plane, or something? Really, Gil, he may not ever leave here, at all."

Patti Hansen is a very beautiful woman, and it was clear that she was asking me to take action, too. Not just Jane.

"Something about the plane?" I asked. "Like there's bad weather coming in, and we'd better make a move soon."

"That would be great," Patti said, eyes flashing.

"Not before the Everly Brothers' tune," I said, somewhat automatically. "He wants to do the Everly Brothers' tune, and he really should. That's next. Don't worry, Patti," I said. "He's really doing fine in there."

"O.K., Gil, that's all great. But what do you think, I mean, what should I tell Jane?"

"Tell her after the Everly Brothers' tune," I laughed.

"O.K., Gil," Patti said, smiling. "You know, you're not bad for forty-one. That's how old you are, right?"

"You read the article in the magazine in the plane?"

"You put it there for us to read."

"Yeah, I guess I did. Listen, don't worry about Keith. I'll get him out of here somehow. Just so long as it's not before we do the Everly Brothers' tune, O.K.?"

"O.K.," Patti said.

I was true to the promise I made to Patti Hansen, although it took me a day or two longer than expected to deliver.

"What d'ya think, Keith," I began. "We've been in here for days, it seems. I've got to do some things in Worcester. You've got to go to Rome. Why don't I call Bill Mahoney, the pilot, and get you and Patti out of here before the front comes through?"

There really was a lot of bad weather on the way, and it's best not to fool around with that unless you really have to.

"Sounds O.K. to me," Keith said. "Sounds O.K. to me. Either that or you've got to give me a job banging nails with those lads out in the barn."

Wouldn't that be something, I mused. Last remaining superstar guitarist knuckles down with North Brookfield country strong hands— building a Sound Stage for the use of his band, the Rolling Stones.

That didn't happen, of course. Instead, we called Mahoney and set up a departure out of Worcester for Teterboro at 11 AM the next morning. And I set about doing some rough mixes of the two-inch recording tape I'd made the night before. The piano demos I'd done with Keith. As luck would have it, our Chief Engineer, Jesse Henderson, had taken a week to do some engineering chores for Sha Na Na, in California. And so I had to engineer myself, leaving Reed Desplaines, Night Manager, to play assistant engineer—running back and forth to the tape library for more reels of virgin tape. This for studio buffs: we used three Neumann '87 microphones on the Steinway, which Pat Metheny left with us two years ago. The piano, I mean. Mikes in our top-secret positions. Another Neumann '87 on him, close up, with a pop filter; voice highly compressed using an Eleven-seventy-six limiter set at twelve-to-one. Finally, a good measure of live acoustic reverb on either side of his voice, in stereo. Lots of E.Q., on everything. I had only one shot at this, and I wanted it to be right the first time.

The live mix was great all by itself, and the best results of that extraordinary session were in fact recorded directly onto our Studer mastering deck, and not the 24-track. 30 ips; no noise reduction, very hot on AMPEX 456 tape.

"Listen to this one, Keith," I said, just before driving him to the airport.

I selected the live stereo tape of "The Nearness of You," a classic Hoagy Carmichael ballad dating from the late '30's. Keith Richards playing the Steinway, and singing, too.

"Far out, Gil. Voice sounds great. Sounds great."

"ZIP—BUZZ . . ." There was a loud, familiar noise on the tape.

"What the hell was that?" Keith asked, with a look of anguish on his face.

"Jane Rose taking a picture of you with her Polaroid camera," I replied.

"Bloody well ruins that take, didn't it?"

"No, Keith," I said. "I think I can razor it out later. We've got this tune about six times, anyway. So don't worry."

Recording enthusiasts will be interested to know that the eventual edits on these ten or so tunes—classic Keith Richards piano demos—took nearly two weeks' work. I found the time to do it only a month after the Stones had finally gone, and performed the edits on a 7½ ips dub inadvertently left behind at my house on Cape Cod. Editing at 7½ ips is no fun, as you may know. Several hundred cuts were required, since Keith never really bothered to begin or end any of the tunes. He'd just keep on playing, and singing, with me scrambling to keep tape on the tape machines, late at night in the A-Control Room at Long View Farm.

Studio A at Long View is the one people travel considerable distances to use, and I think you'd hear it said at the Farm that I can make it work pretty much as well as anybody can. Mixing tape is what I like to do. I can make really good, live, super-present mixes. That's what got me into all this, back in '72, when I was still teaching Philosophy at Clark. I figured I needed some time off to build a studio to make some mixes in. And that's how Long View came about.

So when I tell you that the live stereo tape of Keith Richards sounded good, you better believe me that it did.

We drove Keith Richards and Patti Hansen to the airport the next day. 300-foot overcast; visibility a quarter of a mile in rain and fog. Mahoney couldn't make it in, missing two instrument approaches in an attempt to land 75 X-Ray. So Randall Barbera, who works for me, as you may remember, offered to drive Keith and Patti over to Westfield in the Cadillac. Westfield was still operating, and only about 45 minutes away. They had a wonderful trip, I learned later. Cruising along on a light powdering, Stoli's and orange juice, and a fantastic compilation of fifties rock 'n' roll classics played at high volume on those wonderful-sounding Auratones mounted on the rear deck of the car. Pete Wolf of the J. Geils Band had left this particular cassette behind. By mistake, I'm sure, because it was a real beauty. "Earth Angel," "Good Golly, Miss Molly," "Tears on my Pillow," and songs like that.

"Take this and listen to it on the way to Westfield, Keith. Only remember it's not mine but Pete Wolf's, and he's certain to want it back."

"O.K." Keith said laughing. "I'll bring it back with me. See you."

"See you, Keith," I said.

"Bye, Gil," Patti said, and then they roared off.

And you take it from here, Pete, if you want that cassette back. He won't give it to me.

Let's all pause for a second and note that Keith Richards said "O.K. I'll bring it back with me." Meaning the cassette of course. Meaning also that he intended on coming back to Long View. That this gig was going to happen, after all. It was during Randall's trip to Westfield with Keith Richards that I figured it out all over again—that the Rolling Stones were coming to Long View Farm.

Maybe I'm just a bit slow, sometimes.

It must have been a new moon, or close to it, because the tide was way out, exposing an extra quarter mile of beach, just outside my old Coast Guard boathouse in Truro, on Cape Cod. It was a weekend, a Saturday, and the sun was directly overhead. I had just come down in the Twin, from Worcester.

"Gil, you look terrible."

"Thanks, Bill," I said. Bill's my brother, and had just rented the house up on the bluff for two weeks for himself, his wife, Viki, and his two kids. We were standing on the sandbar—halfway out in the ocean, it felt. Great for kids, let me tell you. Good for big people, too. Particularly somewhat burnt big people.

"I don't feel so good either, if you want to know the truth, Bill. I've been in the control room for three days with Keith Richards. That's what it does to you. Look. Notice the grey pallor to the skin, the bags under the eyes, and the ringing in the ears. That you can't hear—the ringing in the ears—but my ears are ringing, too."

"High volume levels?" my brother asked.

"Yup. Also lots of talk about rock 'n' roll. About other people—half of them dead now, or dying. Lives lost to rock 'n' roll. Decadent, tired stuff. Stayed awake all the time. It was sad in a way. Thrilling in a way. Just happened, you know. Haven't yet figured it out—what exactly happened, I mean. Looks like the Stones are coming to Long View, though. That much looks clear now."

"You just get here?" Bill asked.

"Just now. Haven't seen Nancy or the kids. They been here?"

"About an hour ago," Bill said. "Then she took off down that way with Abby and David. Some other guy with her, too. Don't know who. They all went down that way, towards Brush Hollow."

"Thanks, Bill," I said. I needed some exercise, to get the poisons out of my system. Better than jogging on the road anyhow, low tide was. And so I set off, running along easily on the salt flats, down past the lifeguards and the tourists, south along the beach to the place we call Brush Hollow, and which most new people or visitors call "the nude beach" at Truro.

It wasn't long before I could see them in the distance. That was Nancy, all right. Couldn't tell who it was with her, though. Except for the two little forms, which were almost certainly my kids.

I broke from a jog into a run. Nobody seemed to have any clothes on down there.

About a quarter of a mile away from Nancy—I could tell it was Nancy now, for sure—I see her walk up to where the blanket is, pin her little bathing suit on, and stalk off toward the right, up and over the dune, toward the path that leads through the Hollow and back to the road.

I'm really running now, pounding along at the water's edge, thinking I might still get down there before she disappears over the dune. No way, though. She disappears. Couldn't tell it was me, I figured. So I let off a bit of the steam, dropped back into an easy jog, and thought some thoughts about the Rolling Stones. Much of this book was conceptualized that way. Whenever I relaxed enough to let my mind roam a bit. Whenever I fantasized.

That, of course, is meditation. It's meditation in action; meditation in situation. The repetitiveness of your feet, slamming one after the other into the hard surface of sand, each making a sound like the sound before—like the sound after. It hypnotizes you, and for a second you forget yourself. That's the "window." The window on the future. The person you re-remember is a person with a game plan for tomorrow. A solution to the current dilemma. It's the window that makes the difference. "Zen and rock 'n' roll," if anyone asks you.

Today, running easily along the water's edge, feeling loose, and stronger with each step, it's Keith Richards I'm hearing in my head. It was the song we recorded the night before, or was it two nights before? I don't know. A country tune. Keith Richards singing a country tune with great pain in his voice—great expression. I made the tape play back in my head—something I wasn't able to do at all before turning thirty—and adjusted the speed so it would play along with the sound of my feet on the sand. Keith Richards, loud and live on the studio monitors at Long View Farm; me jogging along a Cape Cod beach under an August sun.

Another great meditation; take it from me. A meditation in situ, which is the best kind; ask any guru.

8 |

THE ROCK SURVIVOR

ROBIN EGGAR | 1983

Robin Eggar's 1983 chat with Richards was for the *Daily Mirror*. That this is a UK tabloid newspaper perhaps explains why the interview is so revealing about things that often get short shrift in the copy of music press journalists eager to assert Richards's edgy credentials, namely love and family.

He has old, old eyes. They have enjoyed great triumphs and indulged in worse squalor. They have seen everything, done everything, travelled to hell and back . . . and survived.

Keith Richards is just a few weeks short of his fortieth birthday. The haggard face is being held back from collapse by force of will.

He could be just another pathetic has-been old pop star junkie.

He chain smokes and tipples Jack Daniels as if it were tea. His voice is slurred, his thought processes appear to ramble.

He shows all the signs of the ex-drug addict searching fruitlessly to replace the one great love of his life—heroin.

But Keith Richards does have replacement loves. He has his band, the Rolling Stones; his fiancee, American model Patti Hansen, his parents and his children.

He also has a throaty, infectious laugh and a caustic wit which quickly slices through his apparent mumblings.

Keith Richards is very much more alive than he has been for the last 15 years.

He has survived everything twenty years at the top of the rock 'n' roll tree can throw at him. And he's proud of it.

Keith says: "I've never regretted going through heroin—especially coming out of it. It made me what I am today.

"I've been through the furnace and out the other side.

"Whether you've got millions or whether you've got nothing heroin is the great equaliser.

"I used to have to go down to Manhattan's lower East Side to score. It's as bad as it can be down there. I'd be carrying a shooter in my pocket.

"Nothing mattered, except getting the dope.

"You only get high the first few times, after that you just maintain the habit.

"The money, the whole way of life you go through to feed it, is so time-consuming and boring.

"But the money wasn't a waste. It was a necessity.

"I'm glad I got out of it," says Richards, draining his whisky glass. "Some of my best friends didn't. Some never will."

The six years since the Mounties entered his Toronto hotel room and arrested him on drugs charges have seen other crucial changes in Keith's lifestyle.

He split with his long-time girlfriend—and the mother of his two children—Anita Pallenberg.

The Rolling Stone who has always refused to gather any marital moss is finally getting married.

"I am going to marry Patti Hansen," he smiles mischievously, "But we've had Mick and Jerry up to here, so I want to let them get it over with first.

"I've only just had the engagement ring made. I'm doing this properly. I'm only doing it once. I'm really old-fashioned that way.

"I presented the ring on bended knee a month ago, in Paris at the Ritz hotel. It was fairly romantic, I can make anywhere romantic.

"Patti and I will have kids eventually. But we've got to find a suitable venue to get married first."

Richards' daughter Angela, 11, lives with her grandmother in England. Marlon, 14, lives in New York with Keith's father.

"The pair of them are terrible together. They go round the local Hell's Angels bars. My dad's got this protector, The Weasel. He's seven foot tall and makes sure they get home safely.

"Dad's 68 and he'd never been on a plane before last year. We only got together then. I hadn't seen him for twenty years.

"I left home 'cos we couldn't live together. After that he separated from my mum and, like a good boy, I took care of her.

"I'm real glad we're friends again. People need their families."

For two decades Richards' only real family has been the Rolling Stones. Like a repentant schoolboy he regrets the heroin days because he let down the band.

If they had ceased to exist back then, he probably would have, too.

"There was never a time when I wanted the Stones to end," he says. "There was for Charlie when his father died just before the 1981 American tour. He was griefed up. We made him keep going to help.

"He hasn't stopped drumming since. He gets better and better—it makes me sick. And Charlie just thinks he's a mediocre jazz drummer.

"We couldn't give Charlie 15 million dollars to continue if he didn't want to. If he stopped I'd stop too.

"But we continue because the Stones aren't as good as they could get. Maybe they never will be."

Richards is adamant that the Stones are still relevant and not just a bunch of ageing, rich rock stars.

"We have always been a mirror of society at the time. Mick is brilliant at articulating the disquiet people are thinking or feeling.

"The new *Under Cover* album has a political feel that dates back to the *Beggars Banquet* era.

"I'm not the person I was in the past. But people won't let me forget. 'He was the junkie. He's still the junkie, the pirate, the rebel, the meanie.'

"In my middle twenties I was confused by my image. I used to wake up in the morning and ask 'Who am I today?' 'Am I the dark side of the Stones mirror?'"

The whisky bottle is empty, the ashtrays full. Keith is still in control. And happy, too. The Stones are still rolling. While he is alive they always will.

"Please spell my name right. With an S," he asks, ancient eyes smiling. "Our manager took it off in the early days to sort of link me with Cliff and the Shads.

"When you're a nobody, that's not a bad deal. And we both survived.

"I know who Keith Richards is now."

9 |

GLIMMERINGS OF IMMORTALITY

BRUCE POLLOCK | 1986

That Keith Richards is a guitar icon and a rock god are givens. Less noted are his contributions to the repository of classic songs. While it is of course understood that he composes, less reflected upon is the fact that he and his collaborator Jagger were, along with John Lennon, Paul McCartney, and Bob Dylan, among the most important songwriters of the 1960s and hence among the most important songwriters of all time. This 1986 interview shines a spotlight on that important quadrant of Richards's talents.

Like a politician on the podium, whistlestopping across the boondocks on a flatbed, Keith Richards has his share of timeless bromides, comfortable answers his tongue slips into after years in the public eye. In the midst of a searing query, or a deft, seven-tiered multiple choice essay question, you can pick them off like sand fleas.

"My first job is to turn the band on."

"When we go into the studio we spend the first few hours just playing the Buddy Holly songbook."

"I have a good feeling about this new album . . ."

"People haven't covered our songs too much, but I take that as a compliment. You don't really hear versions of *Heartbreak Hotel* either. What it means is that your version is pretty much seen as the ultimate."

"More than half the people running record companies are just executives, guys who can sell a whole lot of baked beans. To them a record is just another unit. They couldn't care less about music."

The story about waking up in the middle of the night with the riff for *Satisfaction* is a chestnut, as is his well-documented affinity for the acoustic guitar. "I firmly believe that there ain't a good guitarist around who just plays electric guitar. You can do a lot of tricks on the electric, but as much as I love to play it, a guitarist can keep his chops together on an acoustic, where there's no tricks like sustain. It keeps your wrists and fingers strong. You can't fake it with feedback. You just have to play the thing."

Perhaps his opinion of heavy metal has also made the rounds. "I hate heavy metal," he said. "It just bores me to tears. It sounds like this plane we have in England, with fifteen engines on each wing. It was designed for fantasy. When they built it, it did a great job of charging down the runway, but it never took off."

Certainly you don't think his attitude about the new album, **Dirty Work**, is a freshly-minted burst of enthusiasm, prodded out of him by the reporter's perspicacity or intuition. "Instead of working old formulas here," I noted about the title cut, "it looks like you're adding a few new ones. It could be the sound for the Stones in the 90s." I was falling right into his trap, I sensed, buttering him up with an easy one, but how could I resist? He was such a friendly, elfin sort of guy, smiling at me like a rock 'n' roll Dudley Moore.

"My favorite theme at the moment is that after all these years, rather than marking time, the Rolling Stones are in the unique position of seeing if we can get this thing to grow with us. Rock 'n' roll is just about the same age we are, so nobody's really had the chance to take it this far, not as a band anyway. All of the kings are dead—Elvis, Buddy, Otis Redding. Maybe the most obvious example of how a guy can play a guitar in pretty much the same form as what rock 'n' roll is based on and make it grow up and mature in an interesting way, is Muddy Waters. So for the Stones one of the most interesting things is to see how rock 'n' roll grows up, and see if we can grow it up with us."

So how do you pierce this polished exterior? How do you mine new territory on the much-plowed fields of Rolling Stone history, myth and nuance? The answer proved simple, as obvious as the glimmer in Keith's eyes. So, fans of their rabble-rousing exploits, look elsewhere. Strings and picks fanatics, turn the page. For herein rhythm-cruncher supreme turns orator, nasty scourge of the earth becomes sage, as Keith agrees to expound at length on one of his most overlooked yet favorite subjects: songwriting. With a catalogue of million sellers as vast as it is unrelenting, surely the Stones' output ranks up there with the best that solid rock has produced. No need to give these monsters names, because for twenty years we've welcomed them into our kitchens and bedrooms and hot rods, one after another, chiseled gems of the form, consistently on the mark, lyrically compelling, absolutely rock 'n' roll.

"The hardest thing to write is a really good original rock 'n roll song," Keith said, "because the form is musically very limited. So much depends on the feel and the enthusiasm of the playing. The song is virtually almost an equal partner to the performance. Then there's that indefinable thing that makes rock 'n' roll what it is: that thing that somehow gets in there and nobody knows how."

As a songwriter, Keith Richards is first and foremost a guitarist. "To me songs come out of being a musician, playing. Personally, I cannot write to poetry, rhymed couplets and things like that. I can write a song out of a chord sequence, a riff, and eventually come up with lyrics to fit onto it, but the other way around, no way. The important thing to me is to sit down with an instrument. You might spend three, four hours going through the Buddy Holly songbook, and then out of nowhere there'll be a little crash, and there it goes. All it takes is a split second. It might be an accident, a mistake that sets you off. It's a matter of sitting down and playing, more than with any definite intention to write. All you've got to do is be receptive and recognize when it happens, because it can come from the weirdest angles. Rarely do I write a song totally by myself. Even if I actually do write it by myself, I always like to have someone around just playing along with me, saying, yeah, yeah. I'm a band man, a group man. I can't sit there alone in a room and say, it's songwriting time—ding, ding, ding."

In a very real sense, Keith views the songwriting experience as somewhat metaphysical, although he'd be the last to put such a label on it. "I never think I have to put anything down," he said. "I never care if I have it on tape, or if the tape runs out and the song disappears, because they all come back eventually. I've written songs and lost them and found them ten years later. Once it's there, it's there; it's just a matter of how long it takes before it comes back out again. I find the more I play, the more I'm into it, the more the songs pour out. I don't have a problem with being non-prolific. That's all psychosomatic. Music isn't something to think about, at least initially. Eventually it's got to cover the spectrum, but especially with rock 'n' roll, first it has to touch you somewhere else. It could be the groin; it could be the heart; it could the guts; it could be the toes. It'll get to the brain eventually. The last thing I'm worried about is the brain. You do enough thinking about everything else."

In the studio, Keith relies on the rest of the Stones for valued collaboration. "When we're doing an album, I come in with a handful of riffs and some songs. One or two will be fairly well-defined. Others it would be, this could be dynamite for the Stones, but I have to wait until I get them in the studio and all together in order to really find out. I can't take it any further by myself as a song or a structure or an idea until I've got their input on it. On *Dirty Work*, for instance, we had the hook. The bridge didn't come until we were in the studio trying out various ways of breaking it in the middle, trying to find something that wouldn't be too obvious. I decided, let's just go Jamaican and turn the beat, and suddenly everybody looks around and says, yeah. And that's the way a song is made. It's in the studio that you get those final things that give it something extra."

Songs can also die a death under the caustic glances of his bandmates. "If there's no kiss of life, there's nothing you can do," Keith said. "If everybody walks off to the toilet, then you know you've got to drop that one and go on to something else. But when you just sort of pick up your guitar when the studio is virtually empty, people are telling jokes in the back room or playing dominoes, and then within two or three minutes they drift back, they pick up their instruments and begin whacking away, you know they're into it.

"What a songwriter loves more than anything is a sequence that comes with a hook. Once you get that, you try to expand it. You've got a hook and the first verse, you start to think of the second verse, how to expand the idea. Or do you want to turn it around? Do you want to leave it ambiguous, or do you really want to make a certain kind of point? Bobby Womack and Don Covay have been writing songs even longer than I have. Ronnie has a great tape of them writing songs together one night, and it's ten minutes of chords and a first verse, and then this incredible conversation of: 'Yeah, but she's gonna. . . or, is she gonna be the one with him or is he gonna. . .' And there's a whole soap opera going on. It's like writing a movie script. 'Well, he wouldn't do that because he's got to come back, and that's why you're saying . . .' One of the great things about writing songs is to leave a certain area vague. Even if you're being as specific as you possibly can, somebody else is going to take it totally the other way anyway. It all depends on what they were doing when they heard it."

Keith works differently with Mick than he does with Ron Wood. "When Ron and I sit down together to play, we're two guitarists, whereas with Mick and I there's maybe more of an idea in our heads that what we're after is a song at the end of what we're doing. When Mick comes in with a song, usually he's got it worked out pretty much. He may need a bridge to be written, or a different beat, or turn it around a little bit. Over our whole period, maybe 50% of the time he writes the lyrics and I write the melody. But that's a far, far too simplistic explanation. We write in every conceivable combination of ways. It's really an incredibly elastic arrangement, especially when you're writing with a partner for a band, a specific unit, rather than just writing a song to see who you could sell it to. Some songs hang out for years before we feel happy with them and resurrect them and finish them off. Others, in two takes they've come and gone and you've got to relearn it off your own record to play it later. It happened so quickly you've forgotten how it went. In a way I'm like a guitar maker. Some songs are almost at the end, others are hanging there waiting for that special coat of paint—you can't find the right color for them right now. Lots of times you think you've written four different songs, and you take them to the studio and you realize they're just variations on one song."

These days the Stones have a lot of luxury in the recording studio, the ultimate luxury of using it as a rehearsal hall and sounding board. "When we go into the studio we have to knock the rust off," Keith explained, "because you're either working at top speed or you're training or on the road or in the studio or it's nothing. Nobody ever stops making music, but when you go back in to make an album, the first two months are spent just getting chops and sound together."

In the early days there were different forces moving the industry; in order to even qualify for an album deal, a band had to make its mark in the singles world. Like the Beatles, the Animals, the Who, the Kinks and the Dave Clark Five, the Rolling Stones were first and foremost past masters of the art of the 45: every three months they were required to produce another superior example of the three minute genre made heavenly with the perfect combination of hook and crook.

"I remember after *Satisfaction* got to number one—bang bang at the door. Where's the followup? I mean, every 12 weeks you had to have another one ready. The minute you put out a single you had to start working your butt off on the next one, and the bigger the hit, the more pressure there was on the followup.

"But it was an incredibly good school for songwriting, in that you couldn't piss around for months and months agonizing about the deeper meaning of this or that. It kept you writing all the time. No matter what else you were doing—like touring and recording—you had to make damn sure you didn't let up on the writing. It made you search around and listen for ideas; it made you very aware of what was going on around you— because you were looking for that song. It might come in a coffee shop, or it might come on the street, or in a cab. You get a heightened awareness. You listen to what people say. You might hear a phrase at a bus stop. Instead of accepting life, you start to observe it. You become an outsider rather than a participant. You're listening for it every moment, and anything could be a song, and if you don't have one you're up the creek without a paddle."

For instance, *Ruby Tuesday*. "I saw this picture in some fashion magazine that a chick had lying around her apartment. It was this great photograph of a great chick—she's probably a housewife now, with 15 kids. It was an ad for jewelry—rubies. Also, it happened to be Tuesday. So she became *Ruby Tuesday*. I was just lucky it was Tuesday I guess."

In the sixties the Beatles played Pat Boone to the Stones' Elvis, the essential and elemental rock 'n' roll struggle for good and evil in the minds and hearts of men. The Beatles came to be known as the World's Greatest Songwriters, the Stones as the World's Greatest Band. Off to the side of the fray, the World's Greatest Lyricist, Bob Dylan, lifted the stakes higher.

"I'd say that Lennon definitely felt a strong urge, not so much to compete with Dylan," Keith surmised, "but Bob did spur him to realize he could dig deeper. Mick and I felt that, too, although maybe we didn't feel it as strongly as John. The differences between John and Paul were always greater than between Mick and myself." Keith cited *Sympathy for the Devil* as the Stones' most Dylanesque song. "Mick wrote it almost as a Dylan song, but it ended up a rock 'n roll samba."

But with songs like *Sympathy for the Devil*, *Street Fighting Man*, *Gimme Shelter* and *Stray Cat Blues*, the Stones broadened their bad-boy reputation into a decidedly warped young manhood. To some they were the Devil incarnate. None of this was lost on the Glimmer Twins, as they concocted the image for its greatest benefit. "You use every available tool in the kit," Keith said. "To a certain extent you play on your image. Oh, that's the general perception? And I'd just come up with a line or a song and lean on it, push it, go for it. You get a general feel for what people want to hear from you and when you're good at providing it and they like it— oh, you want more? Here's more. When you first strap on your guitar you just want to play it like so-and-so. Then suddenly you're up there with the spotlight on you and you become aware of the pressures. You have to try and gauge your perception of what you're doing. Nobody writes a song or makes a record to put it in a back drawer."

So although the Beatles and Dylan have catalogues ensconced in the bosom of pop literature, here's a vote for the collected works of the Stones as meriting inclusion on that sacred mount.

"I don't write songs as a diary," Keith said. "None of them are autobiographical, but in some sense they're a reaction to certain emotions. Some of the best songs, some of the happiest ditties in the world come out because you're feeling exactly the opposite. Sometimes you write to counteract that feeling. I was feeling anything but happy when I wrote *Happy*. I wrote *Happy* to make sure there was a word like that and a feeling like that.

"I work best when the sun goes down, I've eaten, had a few drinks, and I've got some good buddies around. I love sitting around with an acoustic guitar and whacking out songs with friends and family. Somehow they never sound as good as they do that first night on the living room couch."

10 |

KEITH ON KEEPING ON

CHRIS SPEDDING | 1986

This 1986 interview with Keith Richards upon the release of the Stones' *Dirty Work* album is surprisingly lacking in references to what Richards termed "World War III": the furious disputes between Richards and Jagger about the latter's solo career that were known to have marked *Dirty Work*'s gestation and would come close to splitting the band permanently. This turns out not to be a demerit as interviewer Chris Spedding finds another entertaining level of communication, speaking English-guitarist-to-English-guitarist with the man radiating the sort of rock iconography that infused Spedding's 1975 UK hit single "Motor Bikin'."

It has to be said that Richards's new mantra—present for neither the first nor last time in this anthology—about using the Stones' unique longevity for the benefit of rock music (". . . see if we can make it grow up with us . . .") has contrasted painfully with the reality of the progressive deterioration of the band's art.

There was a time when the Rolling Stones gleefully played up to a shameless need among certain of their disciples for some kind of hedonistic role model. All very fab 'n' groovy at first, I suppose. Except I have this feeling that the Stones themselves, after a time, must have got heartily sick of it! Just think for a minute . . . These guys have been consistently delivering the right stuff, both on vinyl and in person, for twenty-five years. "The Greatest Rock 'n' Roll Band in the World" is at once both your mandatory show-biz hokum and a prosaic statement of fact.

So I guess it is some kind of tribute to the enduring seductiveness and potency of whatever bizarre tableau they evoke that no one ever stops to ponder how they can possibly still be out there—as prolific, creative and compelling as ever—if they're all supposed to be your lovable ol' burn-outs! Well, that's show business, folks! And I'm sure they must still get a kick out of it.

Now, at this point I'm hoping some of the more perceptive among you will have divined what all this is about. It can mean only one thing. Yes, you got it . . . there's a new Stones album out. Called *Dirty Work* (the first single off it being "Harlem Shuffle"). And since the first hint of a new Stones product usually generates an unseemly stampede throughout all they survey, I must say I find it greatly reassuring that the guys still *care* enough to come out and do the rounds of interviews. They're checking in with us, making contact. Hey, these guys like us!

So on the appointed day, at the highly civilized hour of three-thirty in the afternoon, I presented myself at the Stones' New York office, just a Stones' throw from Columbus Circle. While most of Manhattan was ago-nizing over whether (a) to observe Lincoln's Birthday (b) Valentine's Day counted as a public holiday and (c) we could take the whole damn week off because of the snow, there was none of *that* kind of nonsense at the Stones' office. Very much business as usual.

Keith had phoned ahead with apologies: He'd been delayed leaving the house and would be a few minutes late. A small courtesy, but kind of pleasing in a way. And since the "delay" turned out to be only two or three minutes, it might even score more points than arriving on the dot!

I was shown into a room dominated by a large conference table, the usual vulgar display of framed "platinum" discs refreshingly absent. No need for such ostentation *here*. Wonder where they keep 'em all? Prob-ably in storage until the recording industry designs awards eye-pleasing enough to be worth wall space.

Off in another room a redundant telephone warbled soothingly. One left secure in the knowledge that someone, somewhere, would attend to it.

The door opens. Enter, Keith.

Nattily turned out in a dark blue pinstripe suit, the effect artfully soft-ened by a loosely fitting creamy silk blouse.

Coffee is brought in, and an ashtray for Keith. The scene is set.

So here it is, then. My tête-a-tête with Keith Richards. And a pleasur-able experience it was, too. For me, anyway. Ask the guy a straight question and you get a straight answer. But then, you'd expect that, wouldn't you? I mean, you can't get much more direct, incisive and unpretentious than a Keith Richards riff. It's almost as if the guitar had evolved to the stage where it needed a Keith Richards to come along and reach in and give us a glimpse of part of its true essence, its proto-soul. Keith's unique view of his relationship to his instrument is revealed when he talks (below) of how he first came to ". . . *touch* the guitar." Oh, sure, we've had more flamboyant players who, in varying degrees, have worked the same magic—Jimi Hendrix and Jeff Beck come immediately to mind. But with Keith it's not just a guy playing the guitar; the guitar sometimes appears to be playing *him*—drawing, as he does, on a solid and still-vital blues tradition, sifting and nurturing that rich harvest with just the right sensibilities, thereby becoming the medium—our medium—for its expression, and contributing in the process to some of the more significant songs in our rock repertoire!

The Rolling Stones have carved themselves a sizable niche as the spearhead of a movement that awakened the American consciousness to that neglected part of its own musical heritage—the blues. In this respect their influence has probably been more far-reaching than that of that other flank of the British "invasion," the Beatles. Plus, the Stones are still very much with us!

When Keith spoke of Muddy Waters at the close of our interview, I like to think he was unconsciously expressing hopes for his and the Stones' future.

Chris: So you've just finished a new Stones album, right?

Keith: Yeah. *Dirty Work*.

Chris: Gonna tour?

Keith: Good question. Can't really give you a definite on that. I think so, though.

Chris: Why haven't you done a solo album like other members of the group?

Keith: I've never had a clear enough idea of what I'd want to do. Something's been forming up in my mind over the last three months. Stuff I've just keep shopping around. I say, "Well, there, he sounded good through that. Let's try him through the Bassman. Or the Bandmaster." I mean, you're talking electric guitar. What have you got? You got guitar, you've got your own asshole, and you've got an amplifier. Somehow these three things have to come to be where you want 'em all to be at once. "A Strat might sound good through that Bandmaster, but would the Telecaster sound better through that Champ?" It depends on what sound you're going for. Basically I'm talking recording here, because that's what I've been into for the last year.

For live work, I put the Twin up, and give me Teles and the odd Strat here and there. It's a different criteria. But when you're recording, you never know quite what you're gonna get. The great thing about music is its unpredictability. It never ceases to amaze me. I can be bored stiff—"Oh, man, I wish I had a night off"—and then a little problem will come up, and suddenly I'm in. I say, "How fascinating! Why should that . . . What's the difference between those sounds," and then you see faces light up in the control room. Suddenly you find the right combination, and you're on the track.

You've been described as being able to judge a room's sound just by the snap of your fingers.
Yeah, from echo.

What do you listen for?
The return off of the surface of the room. Where it ends and where it doesn't. You can't tell just by doing that [*snaps fingers*], but you walk around and say, "Well, this is where the drums should go, because we're going to play together in here." You get a bit of information from that, and you look at the size of it and the height. It's almost instinctive; it's not something that you can guide technically and say sure that this is going to work. But you can get a feel within five minutes of walking around a room: Is that a big enough space? Is the ceiling high enough? You give a couple slaps to hear where echo returns from and how quickly it returns. Ambience is one of my favourite things. All the stuff that I cut, whether it's with the Stones or the Winos, it's all room sounds. I've got 10 micro-

phones up in the sky—[*waves arms*] here, there, bring this one in, that one. The room is the important thing.

Has your method for recording acoustic guitar changed since "Satisfaction"?
No, not much. I started making records by saying, "Do I like it? Does this turn me on?" And I refuse to be budged from that criteria. Really. If I start to think about what do they want to hear, then I say I'm out of here. That's not the way I've ever done it. The only times people have liked my stuff is when I've done it because I like it. I'll reserve that for my criteria for anything I do. If I start trying to second-guess people, then I may as well be Liberace or Lawrence Welk. That means I *want* to be a star, instead of having to be forced to be one.

Why do you always play with another guitarist?
Because it's more fun. No one guitar player is that interesting. Not one—I don't care if it's Segovia, Hendrix, anybody. Robert Johnson is the most interesting idea of a solo guitar player to me, and he was looking to go for a band. I'm interested in what I can do with somebody else—how we can interact and play things back and forth and pick up a dropped beat and fling things against the ceiling to see if they stick—and if they don't and fall on your head, you still pick it up. To me, that's the fun of it. And at the same time, you're learning, because you're turning each other on. The solo guitar thing is a vacuum.

With the Rolling Stones, Woody could drop his pick and you'd intuitively cover his part. Do you have a similar relationship with Waddy Wachtel?
Yeah, yeah. I'd known Waddy since the middle '70s, and I've always liked his stuff. Waddy and I have always had that empathy, and he understands my music. I don't have to explain anything to Waddy. That's what you look for, that ESP that doesn't come hard.

That's evident with Steve Jordan, who follows you to a T.
Yeah. I'll drop a beat, he'll pick it up and let it fly. We're playing with time, on this album particularly. But this is like life, right? What is life but play-ing with time? So on a musical level, that's what I'm doing. If you've got

the right guys with you, you can let it flow and get a little daring without being clever. You want to push the edges, and strict time becomes less and less important, since you can always find the one. That obvious structure just gets boring and unnecessary. You say, "Hey, this music can float a little more. I'm gonna use things I learned from Doc Pomus, from Leiber-Stoller, all of that Latin stuff and floating over the lines and leaving out lines and smacking the chorus in your teeth, and then pulling back." Just playing with it is more fun, and that will make it sound more interesting to other people. God knows what I'll do when I get back with the Stones and it's strict time again!

You've sometimes been criticized for turning the beat around.
See, this is what you get from musicians. You're always in this dangerous stall, especially when you've been in the game as long as I have: "What are you trying to do? Turn on the other musicians and give them a little jerk around? Ooh, that's clever." But that's not the name of the game. It's alright jerking around with the time, as long as it all falls in place for Joe Blow. I'm very conscious that a lot of musicians get in this cliquey little thing of turning each other on, and it's all little in-jokes, because you've got nothing better to do except get clever with each other. And it's almost an admission of failure to get into that. I'm very wary of trying to please other musicians.

Your music is not about precision.
No, it's not. It's about chaos. I suppose it reflects my life and probably everybody else's. Nothing happens quite when you think it's supposed to or when you want it to, but when it does, you've got to roll with it. You learn, and you get back up again and pick it up. It's very hard to explain, but I try to do the same thing with the lyrics that I do to the music—a juxtaposition that kind of slams you the wrong way here, and then suddenly it's in the right place. It's just like life.

The music is bigger than all of us. What are we? We're just players, no matter how good. If you're a Mozart or fucking Beethoven or Bach, all you are is just one of the best. If you're an Irving Berlin or Gershwin or Hoagy Carmichael—or if you're Herbie Hancock, God forbid—everybody's got their spot in this. I hate to see music being used as propaganda, which increasingly more it is. But then I think back and realize it always has been—national anthems and signaling [*imitates trumpet flourish*]. When it comes down to it, music evolved out of necessity, not out of pleasure. Somebody got lucky, whipped the other tribe's ass, and then they could use music for fun for a little while because there's no competition. So you get the rockin' down: [*sings*] "We won, we won." You know, so you start to get those songs coming in, apart from just the signaling. And after that, there's this progression.

Music's meaning to people is one of the great mysteries. Forget economics, forget democracy or dictatorships or monarchies. The most fascinating relationship is between people and music and how it can do what it does with no apparent sweat. Who knows what it can do? It's a beautifully subversive language because it can get through anything. I don't care if it's porous or bombproof or has a *Star Wars* shield over it—music will get through. That's my experience.

You've only got to look at the new *Billboard*—who's on the front? Fuckin' Beethoven and Mozart. You can't ask for better than that, boys. Imagine what they'd have done if they'd had a little DAT recorder, instead of all of that imagining it: "Well, that looks good; it might sound great." Those guys had to carry it all up there [*taps forehead*]. Imagine if Mozart and Beethoven had a fucking Walkman! You wouldn't have had 26 overtures, you'd have fifty-bleeding-nine. I mean, those guys would be *green* with envy, man. They would burn their wigs. "Off with it! Burn it! Give me that tape recorder!" [*Laughs.*] What they would have done! They'd have prostituted themselves for one of those things: "No problem! Yeah, give it to me up the ass! Just give me the tape recorder." Go to jail for that shit. And that's where we're lucky, and we can't abuse it.

Have you written any songs lately that seem better suited for the Rolling Stones?
That's a good question, because this leads me to my very point with Mick. In 1985 we started getting into solo shit, and I told him I didn't want to be put into that position after all these years, because I knew it would be

a conflict of interests. I fought him like a dog not to do that. I knew then that I'm gonna write songs and think, "That's mine. Stones can't have that. Oh, the Stones can have this." What do I do? Give 'em the best I got? The second-best? In retrospect now I was right to fear that, but at the same time, the Stones had been in that pressure cooker too long. If you're working with the Stones [*points to a world map dotted with dozens of locations of Stones shows*]—well, that's a year. And then it stops, and you do nothing. And that's what the Stones had to live with from the early '70s until the middle '80s: Constant work for a year and a half, and then nothing for two years. And that stopping and starting was fraying. That was the underlying force of what all of that shit was about. It could have been about women or solo records or quitting smoking or any other thing, but it had to happen. I'm now firmly on my other path as well, and I can see that it's better that I work, Mick works, Charlie, and everybody, so that when we do get together, there's none of this taking the thing off the block and lube jobs.

We'd been too long in that vacuum, in that bubble. You can't live in there forever. The Stones got too big, really, for what the Stones wanted to be. Suddenly you can't just go, "Hey, guys, let's go play down the bar," which is how the band started. It's a strange thing. I wish the Beatles were still around in a way, because they could have kept on doing what they always did first for us, which was open the doors and take the brunt. (*Laughs.*) Playing football stadiums, man, is not where it's at. It takes you into another realm where you don't really want to be. But if that amount of people want to be there, who's gonna say no? So you're, like, stiffed. Give me a 3,000–4,000 seater any time—with a roof on it, no wind, no rain. A good sound system in a controlled environment. Hey, we're rock and roll. What's it need? A basement, a garage. Start from there.

That's the other thing—fame. That can screw you. People come up and ask me about this and that, and I say, "You're talking to a madman." I mean, my view of the world is totally distorted. Since 18, I've had chicks throwing themselves at me, and by a miracle, I turned the little teenage dream into reality like that [*snaps fingers*], God knows how. And therefore my view is gonna be distorted, at the very least.

What's the most dangerous aspect of fame?

Believing it. Very, very dangerous. It's not very good for people around you, and even worse for yourself. That's my experience of it. It's one of the reasons I don't regret zooming into the dope thing for so long. It was an experiment that went on too long, but in a way that kept my feet on the street when I could have just become some brat-ass, rich rock and roll superstar bullshit, and done myself in in another way. I almost forced myself into that in order to counterbalance this superstar shit that was going on around us. I said, "No, I want to put my foot in a deep puddle, because I don't want to hang out up there in that stratosphere with the Maharishi and Mick and Paul McCartney." It was almost a deliberate attempt to get out of it. Like letting the broken tooth hang for five years— deliberate anti! I was doing an anti-gig, but it still stuck. In retrospect, it shouldn't have worked, but that's what I had to do. When I look at it now, that was one of my rationalizations for it. And the other is, hell, I was just sort of into De Quincey's *Opium Eater* a century too late. [*Laughs.*] I just saw myself as a laboratory: "Well, let's see what this does."

Which substances worked best for producing music?

Well, a speedball doesn't go down too bad! [*Laughs uproariously.*] Those were the days. Oh, fuck. You've got the answer there. [*In a loud voice*] A clear mind, a cold shower, and a 10-mile walk after breakfast—those are the ingredients that make good records, not dope.

Bill Wyman once claimed that the Rolling Stones are the only major rock band where everyone follows the rhythm guitarist.

Well, that's the best thing he's ever said about me! [*Laughs.*] He never told me that. Bill, bless your heart. I just hope he's there to follow me the next time around. Which leads us to that question, right? Whether or not he's in the band is up to him. As far as I'm concerned, there's no way I want to change that lineup, unless he's absolutely adamant. I have my spies out. I talk to his ex-old ladies, who can see him. Some people tell me he means it, and then I speak to some of his older friends who have a feeling he'll be there. So I'm getting these two messages. And Bill is not the guy . . . We don't talk on the phone, because he's too guarded and I'm too pointed. I have to see his eyes to know. It was a spin on my head when I discovered he just doesn't like flying anymore. Hell, you can't think of everything. There's all kinds of angles and possibilities on this thing with Bill, but I don't want to change this lineup unless I really got to. And he's the only one that can make me have to. Playing guitar is one thing, playing the other guys is another. I realize that more and more as I go ahead. Hey, I've become a psychologist over the years. I do it almost automatically.

Many people have mimicked your image and attitudes. What would you have musicians learn from you?
Forget about the clothes and the haircut and the moves, and then concentrate on the guitar playing. First, you've got to have that. I see a lot of guys out there—and it's like weird for me—and they've got it all down except the playing! [*Laughs.*] I mean, hell, they look more like me than me! It's like fashion. It's all got to do with video and shit. Once you start to get the eyes involved with music, music will take the back seat, and that's what the video thing is. Why can't video find its own niche in life and get off music's back? This is not going to endear me to VH-1 or MTV, but they know how I feel about it. It's a confliction of the senses. You're gonna judge a record by a TV screen and some images with some shitty little sound coming out of those boxy little speakers? The way they deliver a record is with some semi-nude chicks, which I have no problem with, but not to sell my music. The music becomes like elevator background music, relegated. And of course, then you've encouraged people to become poseurs and not composers. Andy Warhol's little dream's come true: Everybody's a star for 15 minutes.

Music, to me, is the joy, right? I love my kids most of the time, and I love my wife most of the time. Music I love all the time. It's the only constant thing in my life. It's the one thing you can count on.

15 |

STONES KEEP ROLLING

ROY TRAKIN | 2002

This being a book of Keith Richards interviews, Mick Jagger is usually mentioned only in passing. However, an exception has been made for this interview twinset, whose timing and content irresistibly provides a window onto how the two men have gone their separate philosophical ways over the years. Once so united in their defiance of convention that their joint imprisonment was perfectly symbolic, Mick and Keith have grown so much apart that in 2002 Jagger did something Richards would sooner die than contemplate: accept a knighthood. However, it's more than that. Richards seems now as warm and approachable as Jagger seems uninterested and uptight. To be fair, Jagger has to be admired for the way he has always refrained from succumbing to the temptation to be as publicly scathing about Richards's considerable failings as the latter has been about his. However, conducted only three months after the announcement of Jagger's acceptance of a knee-dip, these parallel conversations speak volumes about the now insuperable differences between the self-styled "Glimmer Twins."

In conversation, Rolling Stones founders Mick Jagger and Keith Richards couldn't be more different. Jagger is diplomatic, political, professional, making sure he doesn't offend a single potential Stones buyer, and filled with bonhomie, but chilled to the bone and easily bored. On the other hand, Richards is exactly how you see him, cigarette cocked between his lips, leaning up against Ronnie Wood, truly the salt of the earth, ready to say anything about anybody, listening and responding, giving you all the time you need, a real person.

A study in contrasts, Jagger and Richards are rock's greatest living duo—the heart and soul of the Rolling Stones for going on four decades now. They're celebrating the milestone with a number of high-profile projects, including the Oct. 1 release of their own greatest-hits answer to the Beatles' *1*, Virgin/EMI's *Forty Licks*. The set also features four new songs recorded with producer Don Was in Paris, including the first single, the aptly named "Don't Stop." In addition, Allen Klein's ABKCO has just re-released the band's entire pre–*Sticky Fingers* catalog—22 albums in all—in SuperAudio CD that have old fans raving at the meticulous re-mastering, which makes the discs sound like they were recorded yesterday.

Mick and Keith were in Toronto, where they recently played a warm-up gig at the Palais Royale prior to the launch of their massive Licks tour, which got underway this week (9/3) at Boston's Fleet Center. They were hoodwinked into spending some valuable phone time with *HITS*' stalker Roy *"Well You Heard About the Midnight Tummler"* Trakin.

PART 1: MICK JAGGER

The Toronto warm-up show sounded fantastic.
Mick Jagger: It was good fun. Some bits were better than others. [Laughs] It went really good.

The set list was pretty interesting. Is it close to what we can expect on the tour?
I don't know what we're going to do. It depends on the place we're playing, the town we're in.

So there'll be different sets depending on the size of the venue in each city.
That's the way I see it, really. In the cities where we're doing three venues, I see the theaters as much more the place to do songs that aren't perhaps so well-known.

For the real fans.
It's not so much that they're more real; they're no more real than anyone else. It's just easier in a small place to play what you like. You can hear

better. It's just more suited to experimentation. It's not so much of a show as a musical performance. The bigger it gets, the more of a spectacle it is. In an arena like the Garden, you have to strike a good balance between well-known material and something that's not quite as popular. And in a very, very big stadium, I think you have to veer towards the well-known. I think that's what works. You don't want to play too many mystery numbers in a stadium.

So you've been in Toronto this whole time?
Yup. Just playing, doing a whole bunch of songs. Last 10 days, we've been trying to narrow things down a bit. Getting the set lists together. [Laughs] It sounds good.

Is playing together like riding a bicycle for you guys at this point? Do you just jump back on and start peddling?
Some of it feels like that. But we had quite a lot of things to work out. If you're only going to do 22 songs, then it would be easy. But if you're trying to get a repertoire of, say, maybe 60–70 songs, that's quite a lot to remember. And there's a lot to go wrong.

Is it still as much fun for you as it's always been?
It was good to do the show the other night. It gives you a more realistic feel. Otherwise, you're stuck in a rehearsal room. Once it gets outside of there, it becomes much more real and more fun. You get feedback from an audience as to how they like one number over another. I mean, that's what you're doing. You're not doing it in isolation.

I noticed in the Toronto set list some chestnuts you really haven't played for awhile, like "Heart of Stone."
I can't remember when we played that one last. Years ago. Sounds a bit different now.

How did you go about putting together this greatest hits record?
First thing I wanted it to be was the most famous songs from the beginning to the present-day. Then I just threw in a few more favorites that

maybe weren't singles, but songs that have been played alot and people have always liked. And then, we wanted to put some new songs in, so we went to Paris to record. We ended up with four new songs and a whole lot more material we'll work on later.

Why did you decide to put out a best-of record at this point rather than a whole new album?
I thought it was good to put together this package, which had never been done. I'd hoped to put it together for a while, but I was ready to forget it, basically. But it seemed like a great time to get a whole overview of everything from early '60s to present-day.

You and Keith appear to be in mid-tour form with some of the exchanges going on between you about the solo album and your knighthood.
I don't do sniping.

When are you getting knighted?
I haven't heard anything about it since I got the first letter.

Keith said you shouldn't have settled for just a knighthood.
I don't do sniping. I told you that. So you can't get me to do it.

I was just curious about your take on being knighted.
It's a very nice thing to have. I mean, it's nice to be asked [laughs]. But it's something you should wear lightly. Understand what I mean? You shouldn't make a big deal about it. You shouldn't ram it down people's throats . . . or put on airs or graces. You should just accept it as a nice compliment.

Were you disappointed in the sales performance of your last solo album, *Goddess in the Doorway*?
Well, I think we did pretty well. We sold well over a million worldwide. We had a record company that was self-destructing in the United States. Which is still in the process of picking its pieces up. [Laughs] I know because I'm still on it. Outside the U.S., we did quite well. We did Top Five

in Europe, which I think is good. In a lot of territories, we did as much as *Bridges to Babylon*. In America, two-thirds of the company was fired the day the record came out. [Laughs] It wasn't very good timing.

What's your take on the current disputes between artists and labels here in the States?
There's always been trouble, ever since year one. We used to have tremendous rows with our first record company [Decca], who were completely hopeless. They just didn't get it. One of the problems is, record companies cut costs. I'm not a great expert on this; I'm just kind of guessing. But as they cut costs, they employ fewer people that really have any rapport with artists at all. And people end up with lots of different jobs to do that they're not necessarily suited for, but are only too happy to do. I think that communication just gets completely broken down. Virgin was in a process of complete reorganization. They couldn't manage to sell the company, so what were they going to do next? And you get caught in the middle of that, even though it has nothing to do with you, to be perfectly honest. If you're caught in that, you can say they didn't promote the record properly. Trouble is, those people are more worried about keeping their jobs than promoting your record.

You may be one of the few bands with enough brand recognition to do break away from the major-label system.
I think that's definitely something to think about in the future. We all know the music business has shifted a lot. Music's evolving into lots of other formats. It's in a different place. I'm sure it's still exciting for some people, but putting out CDs doesn't seem to be quite the event it used to be . . . for various reasons. Wouldn't you agree? One has to reconsider the whole thing of recorded music and its distribution, but everybody is starting to.

So far, there hasn't been too much talk about this being the last Stones tour.
I think people have just gotten fed up asking. I mean, I have had that question. I always give the same boring answer, which is just sort of exis-

tential. Without even starting the tour, we could all get killed in a bus. You never know what's going to happen. You can't tell the future.

I just read your former manager Andrew Loog Oldham claims in his autobiography he once slept in the same bed with you.
I can't talk about my affairs from 50 years ago or something. This is a music magazine, isn't it?

What about your own autobiography? Haven't you been working on that for years?
That was 15 years ago. That's really old hat. I don't wanna go there. Are we almost finished now? Thank you very much. It was nice talking to you.

PART 2: KEITH RICHARDS

Have you been keeping track of the turmoil in the U.S. record industry these days?
Keith Richards: Of course. Things like EMI going, like, *doink* . . . I mean, we've worked with these people, off and on, all our lives. They're as true and blue as the British Empire and all of that. Changing times, man. They were living far too high and far too fat for far too long, ya know?

All the musician wants to do is play and record, but you guys seem to have taken care of business through the years.
We don't get involved to that extent. We make our deals and then we fulfill 'em. The difficult thing has been in the area of promotion. You have to argue how much they're going to put into this, and who's radio's favorite flavor of the month. And it kinda gets a little tacky. But it always has been. It's always been a pool of piranhas, and they always wore sharkskin suits.

I just read Andrew Loog Oldham's autobiography. It was a much different world back then, more innocent.
It was real. I remember our first record deal with Decca. We were in the boardroom with Sir Edward whatever-his-name-was, who was 80 years old and drooling. Actually, it was like a *Sopranos* thing. He was wearing

shades he didn't take off. And then he let us do what we wanted [laughs]. The first thing we did was lease tracks to them. We didn't sign a contract. Which was a famous deal. I'm glad we did it that way because that meant we had the all-important "artistic control."

I always know when you guys are getting warmed up for a new tour because the sniping in the press heats up.

Most of the energy has been very positive, real good. Usually, it takes a few weeks to knock off the rust. But I don't know . . . They've come in well-oiled, man. It's really sounding good. The only down side was the death of [longtime roadie Roydon] Chuch McGee. He's one of the pillars that kept the Stones up, though you never saw him. He had a heart attack a couple of weeks ago, which sobered everybody up.

What was your reaction to John Entwistle's death?

That was another surprise. Isn't it amazing, just before the first show of the tour . . . I didn't know him well. I don't know if anybody did, really. I'm sure he had a lot of close friends. I'd known him for so long. And he always sent me some nice notes. He was a very quiet man, ya know. When you get taken, man, you get taken. But it didn't stop Roger or Pete. I heard they got my old friend Pino [Palladino] on bass. And the tour must go on . . .

So no Bill Wyman again this time around?

No, no. I got a message from him just a couple of weeks ago. Now and again, we get in touch. Otherwise, he's too busy having babies. It's something he's good at. Since he left the Stones, he's had about three daughters. That's his favorite occupation.

Has he discovered Viagra?

Bill's always been like that. That's why he's so fuckin' skinny, man [laughs].

You recently put down Mick's solo record in the press.

I mean, where else could you put it? When they asked me about it, I said, "Oh, you mean *Dogshit in the Hallway*?" The quibble with that is Mick had told me months and months before he was not going to do any solo projects and we were going to concentrate on getting this thing together. And then suddenly, his dogshit appears. And then I heard it, and I thought, "Yeah, it is dogshit."

And what about his whole knighthood thing?
I really flared up about that. I thought it was really stupid timing. Typical of Mick to break rank. I mean, right now, he could have done himself a lot better by turning it down.

You're anti-royalist?
Well, I'm not "anti." I just think people like Frankie Drake and Wally Riley deserve knighthood. I don't really see what pop singers have to do with it. But if they do, it's a bit of a paltry honor, innit? If Phil Collins is a knight, then you should hang out for the fuckin' peerage, man. Get a Lordship. They give knighthoods for covering a few Supremes songs.

So we're never going to have a Sir Keith Richards.
I very much doubt it. I'm too vocal. And also, I always thought Mick was, too. But I told him, "Now you've joined the brown-noses."

Have you heard any of the remastered titles?
Allen [Klein] sent me a copy of them. Very good mixes. Some very interesting work has been going on there.

It's like hearing these old songs for the first time.
To me, too. This new system of re-mastering and re-mixing them amazed me, too. [Laughs] I was hearing instruments I forgot I put on there. It's amazing what's on tape and what can be pulled out.

Have you watched *The Osbournes*?
No, I haven't. I wasn't in the country when it was on. It sounds like exactly what Ozzy needs. Ozzy's always going to pull something out of his hat every now and again. And that was a good one, I think. Ya know, it's kinda like *The Simpsons*, but live.

Have you ever considered a reality show yourself?
No way, man. Reality's enough without being virtual.

What do you think about this new garage-band punk movement? The Hives have a singer who looks like a young Mick Jagger.
[Mock sneer] What's so new about it? I'm not surprised because that's what they should be doing. Also, because last time we were on the road, five years ago, those 12-year-olds in the front row are now 17, 18 and they're rocking. A lot of these guys are my tribe, in one way or another. Even if they don't know it.

And now you're putting out a greatest hits album, like the Beatles' *1*.
The only difference between the Beatles and us is we're still going. So we thought it was necessary and important to at least put on some new tracks. Like a dot-dot-dot . . . To be continued, so to speak.

Keith, how long can this keep going?
[Incredulous] You're asking *me*? We've never said anything about it being the last time. It's always from the outside. Including now. I think they've just thrown up their hands in disgust and said, "We can't use the bit about it being the last tour anymore. It doesn't work. They keep coming back."

You always seem to have a good time.
Pursuit of happiness, man. It's in the Constitution. You don't have to be a rocket scientist to figure out that, if you're miserable, it's really miserable. The only other side of the coin is, enjoy it. Figure it out. It ain't that difficult. Some people just look for trouble and want it and other people just deal with it.

Do you go for medical check-ups regularly?
We have to do all of that to get insurance for the tour. The last report I got, I was 38 and didn't smoke. And I said, "I'll take that, doc." [Laughs]

So you haven't had one of these colonoscopies yet, where they put a camera up your butt?

What the fuck would people do that for?

When you're over 50, you're supposed to get one, to check for colon cancer.

Horse shit. They did all that crap. I have a very unexcited prostate, if you wanna know. And that's the way we like it.

You'll end up dancing on all our graves.

I dunno, man. That's not a pleasant thought. Where does that leave me, ya know? [Laughs]

16 |

KEEF

JAMES MCNAIR | 2005

The year 2005: another Stones world tour, another rehearsal period located in Canada for tax purposes, another round of publicity to drum up interest. Despite the familiar circumstances, James McNair found Richards an entertaining and revealing interviewee—even though it is immediately evident that it was by now impossible for "Keef" and any interviewer to have a conversation not layered with self-consciousness about the guitarist's über-hedonist image.

So the Grim Reaper is sitting at home watching TV when the doorbell rings. He opens up and Keith Richards is standing there in hooded black sackcloth, a sharp-looking scythe at his side. "Sorry," says the Rolling Stones' seemingly indestructible guitarist. "Your number's up."

Presented with the above vignette, Richards gets the joke. "Yeah, I'd like to see the Reaper off," he says with a gruff laugh, "but people shouldn't try and do what I've done with my body, because not everybody can." As though to underline that truth, he swigs at a large vodka and orangeade-based concoction called a Nuclear Fall-Out. Would I like to try one? No, I'll stick with beer, thanks.

Sixty-two in December, Richards is enjoying his tipple while chain-smoking full-strength Marlboros. Though it's only 5.30pm, his skulls-and-guitars-appointed dressing room is candle-lit. The air is heavy with incense, and a small, coffin-shaped box on the table lies open to reveal Keith's rolling papers. He's wearing lime-green work boots, and a black tracksuit top with the word "Jamaica" emblazoned in yellow on the back.

You take in his gnarly knuckled fingers, his swarthy, heavily latticed face. On his right hand is the familiar silver skull ring that he has long worn as a *memento mori*. Keith's eyes are so brown they are almost black, and juju trinkets dangle from his gloriously unkempt hair. An amiable rogue who has been described as "a grinning baboon" and "the human riff," the guitarist proves surprisingly well spoken. As the vodka kicks in and he starts to slur a little, he puts me in mind of Rowley Birkin, the genial, dipsomaniac QC from *The Fast Show*.

"I went to see my dentist the other day," Richards says, still on the topic of his rude good health. "Chipped tooth. Hadn't seen him in 20 years. He thought he'd put me out on anaesthetic, but he hadn't—I was just sitting there feeling pleasant with my eyes closed. First I hear him praising his own handiwork; then he starts rooting around with his dental tools. After a bit I hear, 'This guy's immune system is fucking unbeliev-able!' I chuckled to myself but didn't say anything."

Richards' dressing room is stationed within Greenwood College School. It is here, incongruously, in a quiet suburb of Toronto, Canada, that the Rolling Stones are once again rehearsing for an upcoming US tour. Richards' manager, Jane Rose, is on site, as is her tiny white Mal-tese, Ruby Tuesday, so named by Keith himself. On closer inspection the pooch is seen to be wearing a leopard-print scrunchy.

By Richards' account, rehearsals are going well: is contemplating the 43-date August-January tour like contemplating Everest?

"No, it's like downhill skiing! Nobody is dragging their ass to come on this one." Even Charlie Watts, traditionally the most touring-reticent Stone, can't wait to get going—and this despite the drummer's recent bat-tle with throat cancer. "Charlie's fine now and he came back firing on all cylinders, maybe to prove a point," says Richards of his 63-year-old col-league. "If that's what chemo does for you, I'm going in for some."

Later, when I sit in on the Stones' rehearsal session, it's clear that Richards' claims about the camp's high morale are valid. It's fascinating to watch the group in something like private, Keith perusing the set-list through dainty pince-nez while he and 58-year-old Ronnie Wood's gritty guitars spar to glorious effect. Mick Jagger—62, black baseball boots *sans* laces, 28-inch waist still intact—looks almost boyish as he beams at backing vocalist Lisa Fischer during "Gimme Shelter." When he catches sight of me on the balcony he does a double take, however—the thought bubble above his head reading: "Who let *him* in?"

If the Stones' appetite for their upcoming jaunt is tangible, Richards, for one, was less enamoured with the notion of Live8, and actually vetoed the idea of the Stones playing the event. "I didn't understand why everybody who was trying to coax me in happened to be knighted," he says with a laugh. "I got hit on by Sir Bob and Sir Mick, but I said to Mick, 'We ain't doing it, pal. *You* can do it, but I ain't.'

"Decreasing debts?" the guitarist goes on. "It all seemed a bit nebulous to me. Plus I couldn't believe the amount of pressure, even from 10 Downing Street. I was like, 'We're finishing the new album and getting ready for the tour—sorry, but we can't spare the men.' I heartily applaud what they were trying to do, except that it was tied in with Government policy and I always try and separate politics and music. I mean, Bob's a nice bloke and all that, but ultimately he's the one who comes off best, isn't he?"

The new album Richards mentions is *A Bigger Bang*, due in September. It's the group's first studio outing since 1997's *Bridges to Babylon*, and as its title suggests, it sees the world's greatest extant rock band shirking complacency and roaring loud. Not every track is a classic, it's true, but "Laugh, I Nearly Died" is as agreeably raunchy as anything on *Sticky Fingers*, while "Rain Fall Down" is the band's funkiest moment since 1983's "Undercover of the Night."

Elsewhere, on the flagship single "Streets of Love," an uncharacteristically lovelorn Jagger delivers one of the most compelling performances of his career, his diction masterful and his ad-libs on the fade-out unmistakably heartfelt. Lyrically, it's one of several songs on the new record that have led some to posit that the work is partly Jagger's love-letter to his estranged wife, Jerry Hall. "The awful truth/Is really sad/I must admit/I was awful bad," sings the old philanderer at one point. It sounds awfully like he's acknowledging his costly dalliance with a 20-year-old Brazilian lingerie model by the name of Luciana Morad (in 1999, Morad bore Jagger a child; Hall filed for divorce shortly afterwards).

With Charlie recuperating and Ronnie Wood facing equally testing times (the guitarist was devastated when his first wife Krissy took her own life earlier this year) Richards says he and Jagger were forced to pull their fingers out on *A Bigger Bang*.

"We were short staffed," he quips, enjoying a quotidian phrase and deliberately sounding like himself as caricatured by John Sessions on *Stella Street*. "Mick and I got the news that Charlie was going in for treatment just as we started writing. There was a pregnant pause, and we thought, 'Should we put things on hold?' But then it was, 'No, let's forge ahead—it will be a good incentive for Charlie. Actually, this is probably the closest Mick and I have worked together since *Exile on Main Street*. Both of us took on tasks that normally wouldn't have occurred to us, playing bass or whatever.

"Mick playing great guitar helped," Richards continues. "I sleep downstairs and the studio is upstairs. One night I thought I was hearing this old Muddy Waters track I didn't know, but it turned out to be Mick working on a slide part for 'Back of my Hand.' He's always been a good, smooth acoustic player, but the electric seemed like an untamed beast for him until this year. When I heard him this time I thought, 'My God! The boy's finally got it.'"

This is how Richards goes on: holding court, spinning anecdotes, and generally leaving no buckle unswashed. No huge surprise, then, that he has reportedly been offered a part in *Pirates of the Caribbean III* (*Pirates II* is already in the can). While his pal Johnny Depp famously used Keith as a template when playing the roguish Jack Sparrow, Richards says he can neither "confirm nor deny" his own involvement in the trilogy.

"What I can tell you," he says, "is that when we were finishing the album in LA, Johnny came down to the studio to talk about the movie. Behind him was, like, the Disney wardrobe department or something, and we spent the rest of the afternoon hilariously dressing up in pirate clothes. I'm up for doing the film and so is Johnny, so hopefully we can schedule something in . . . I'd obviously bring my own cutlass, ha ha!"

Joking aside, this last is not a fact that anyone who knows Keith Richards would doubt. Ask director Julien Temple: before he worked on the 1983 video for "Undercover of the Night," Richards reportedly flicked open a switchblade, held it to Temple's throat and said, "You better not fuck up."

My host's liking for firearms has been well documented too, but he says that these days he leaves his handgun in the drawer at home. When he was scoring dope in the US in the late 1960s, however, he carried one around as a matter of course. "I'd read that Muddy Waters had one, and I suppose there was a bit of emulation going on there. America was a strange, lawless place back then. You'd be in some motel, and people would be shooting at each other, but unfortunately you'd be in the room in between. I used to keep my gun under my pillow [laughs], but then it becomes like your fetish, and you can't go to sleep unless it's there. Then you start wondering what you're worried about and if you'd actually use the gun anyway. I got pretty good at light bulbs and chandeliers, though. You had to check it was still working."

Asked what the biggest misconception about him is, Richards is stumped for a few moments. The public face of Keith Richards, he says, is a caricature with a large element of truth in it. "I've been cast in the role of the rascal and I accept the role gracefully," he laughs, "but everybody changes. The problem is that, when you've been famous for this long you drag all the key events and rumours of your life around with you like Jacob Marley's chain."

For Richards, these would include the night he wrote the riffs for "Satisfaction" and "Brown Sugar," the bloodbath that was the Rolling Stones at Altamont in 1969, the mysterious death of Brian Jones earlier that same year, and the persistent myth that a Swiss blood transfusion process akin to premature embalming was what enabled Keith to temporarily kick heroin prior to an important, 1973 tour of Europe. The mere mention of the latter proves enough to help Richards find an answer to my previous question. The biggest myth about him, he now posits, is probably that he was constantly endangering himself with drugs. "Actually, I would take drugs quite responsibly," he says. "A nice fix at breakfast, one for elevenses, and another one at teatime—it was like breaks at the cricket, or something.

"The times I fucked up was when I scored from people I didn't know and the stuff was laced with strychnine. I'm lying on the bed, and people are going, 'Well, he's still breathing . . .' It was a bit Edgar Allen Poe-ish; a bit like being buried alive. You could hear every word they were saying, but you couldn't say anything back because you were paralysed.

"John Lennon did that, too," Richards goes on. "He seemed to be in competition with me over drugs, and I never really understood that."

Was he a Rolling Stone in Beatles clothing?

"That's interesting—you might have something there. I think the Stones behaved like he'd like the Beatles to behave, and [because of that] he felt constricted."

Richards' main home is still in Weston, Connecticut, and he continues to share it with Patti Hansen, the Staten Island–born model whom he married in 1983. It was at home on the couch that Keith penned "This Place Is Empty" [without you], a fine country-style ballad from the new album that he croons raggedly *à la* Tom Waits. The guitarist concedes the song was partly written for Patti (one great line runs: "Come on, honey/ bear your breasts/and make me feel at home"), but the lyric's wider resonance may take in empty-nest syndrome.

"Our daughters, Theodora and Alexandria, have grown up and got their own apartment in the city," he says. "For a while we didn't know what to be doing, but then Patti said, 'Jesus Christ! We can do want we want! Let's be a couple again, darling!'"

There are also grandchildren to enjoy, these fathered by Keith's son, Marlon, who together with Angela, his other child by Anita Pallenberg, is now well into his thirties. "Marlon's got little Ella, bless her heart, and Orson, who's about five now," says proud granddad. "Thanks to Johnny [Depp], Orson actually thinks I'm a real pirate. He's coming up just nicely, learning all the right cuss words."

Clearly, Richards is in fine fettle. He's already had three Nuclear Fall-Outs, but this has merely whetted his appetite for the rehearsal session that will begin immediately after our chat. What, though, of absent friends and family? Richards has lost Brian Jones, and his own father, Bert. He has lost musical soulmates such as country star Gram Parsons, and the Rolling Stones' unofficial extra member and keyboard player, Ian Stewart.

As his own pension book looms closer, are there moments when Keith recalls these people? Does he dream of them, perhaps?

"They come and visit now and then, and not necessarily when I'm asleep. I'll be talking away to someone and Bert will come in and say, 'A fox never shits in his own hole, Keith!' Parsons sometimes comes to me in dreams, but that's more of a musical thing. Ian Stewart? Man, he just rings like a bell. Whenever one of us in the band tries to pull a number, somebody will drop a little Stu-ism like, 'Come along my little shower of shit.' These people resonate; you never forget them. I miss all those cats."

And Brian? Is it all just too long ago now?

"Brian could be the most frustratingly obnoxious, nasty person. Which he never was until the minute we had a hit record. It was a fame thing, maybe; something seemed to snap in him. It could be that he thought he was *numero uno* and Mick didn't like that. I wasn't thinking about hierarchy at the time—I was just trying to find [the chord of] E7.

"We were pretty mean to him. We started to pick on him just to let him know: either you're in or you're out. And then he got more and more stoned, and he'd check into a clinic in Chicago while we were touring the Mid-West. I'm standing on stage trying to cover two guitar parts—it doesn't endear you to the guy.

"Later, I made a real effort to hang with Brian. This would be '66–'67, when we finally got off the road for a year. Everybody's getting stoned out of their brains and there's acid flying about. We were having a good time, but unfortunately there was Anita [Pallenberg—Jones's girlfriend before Richards "rescued" her from him], and then we get into that. That was the final nail in the coffin."

At that, our time is up. One last question, though: does he have any kind of fitness regime prior to going on the road? "Yeah," he deadpans, "It's called 'Rehearsals.'"

"Mick's your guy for a fitness regime and a schedule," he adds, "but then he has to cover a lot more stage than me.

"When I wake up in the morning I just say, Ahh! Jah wonderful! Let's see what the day brings! I'm happy to be here. I'm happy to be *anywhere*."

17 |

KEITH RICHARDS AND THE MAKING OF *EXILE ON MAIN ST.*

PIERRE PERRONE | 2010

When the Rolling Stones released their only double studio LP, *Exile on Main St.*, in 1972, it was greeted with reviews that mostly ranged from negative to lukewarm. By the time Richards was helping promote a deluxe remaster of the album thirty-eight years later, it had long been widely reassessed as a classic, even the band's magnum opus.

This interview with Pierre Perrone about *Exile*'s genesis is not just absorbing. It is a salutary reminder that though Richards is a candid interviewee and projects a devil-may-care attitude, he is also intelligent and business-savvy enough to know when to deploy discretion, for something else that had occurred in the thirty-eight-year interim was the settling of the Stones' legal disputes with their former manager Allen Klein, which meant that Richards was no longer obliged to stick to the story he and his colleagues had maintained for many years that the album's basic tracks were recorded exclusively in Richards' South of France basement.

Thirty-eight years on from its original release, *Exile on Main St* is the stuff of rock'n'roll legend, many people's favourite Stones album and the one Keith Richards is always happy to return to. So much so that the Glimmer Twins, who are notoriously loath to open up the vaults, have finally assembled a deluxe edition with 10 bonus tracks on top of the 18 first issued in 1972.

I've followed the Stones since I was a kid. I covered their songs in a garage band and failed exams because I travelled to see them in Nice the night before. I've seen them live over a dozen times, in France, in London, in the US. Three years ago, I wrote the liner notes for the re-release of the *Rolled Gold+* compilation. Over the years, I've interviewed Mick Jagger, Charlie Watts and Ronnie Wood, but never Keith Richards.

I'd resigned myself to his glaring absence from my lengthy list of interviewees until the expanded, remastered *Exile*, an ideal opportunity for a kid who spent half of 1971 dreaming of running away from Marseilles to join the Stones at Nellcôte, in Villefranche-sur-Mer.

Richards is tickled when I tell him this. He's at the Mercer Hotel, a luxury establishment in New York, the Big Apple's equivalent of LA's Chateau Marmont. No one bats an eyelid when he lights up. The old devil.

Fans are pretty excited at the prospect of the remastered, expanded *Exile on Main On St* coming out. What has it been like for you to listen back to the tracks?

A lot of déjà vu. There was a point where I was listening to it all and remembering where it was recorded, Villefranche-sur-Mer and old Nellcôte. I could almost smell the basement. I still like the album and often play bits of it. I've fond memories of making the record. It was a little crazy and, in a way, unique, because we'd never recorded outside of a studio before, so this was a bit of an experiment. But, once we started, it had to be finished.

Bands such as Traffic used to rent a cottage and get it together in the country, but you actually recorded in a basement in a villa on the French Riviera. What was the chain of events that led you to Nellcôte?

The full weight of the British establishment came down on us. First they thought they could get us with the dope busts and it did not work, so they put the financial screws on. To keep the band going, we had to leave England. France was convenient. At first, we figured that either in Cannes, Nice or Marseilles, maybe we could find a studio that we liked. But, when we got there, we realised it was out of the question. Then it was a matter of finding a house in the hills somewhere but, after that fell through, everyone suddenly looked at me (*laughs*). I thought: 'I know what they want, they want my basement.' That's how it ended up. I lived on top of the factory.

You already had The Rolling Stones Mobile Studio. You'd used it for live recordings and at Stargroves, Mick's place. The Who used it too. And Led Zeppelin later on.

Yeah. We'd had the truck for a couple of years. I can't remember quite how long. We'd never used it very much ourselves. We used it to cut a few demos. We used to rent it out to the BBC or somebody to do the race courses. But suddenly I realised, I think we all did, that we did have this mobile control room. Having that made it possible. The thing actually worked. We were amazed. It was a lovely machine, for its time. When we did put that truck together, we thought that it might come in useful. And sure enough it did.

There was quite a vibe in that basement, wasn't there?

Yes, you can call it a vibe, it was a thick one (*laughs*). It was a unique place to work. Upstairs, it was a fantastic place. The basement was another story. We had to sort of get around all kinds of problems, sound-wise and. . . But there was a certain determination in the band that, OK, we had to leave England. We can do what we do anywhere. There was a lot of determination in the band to step up to the plate and make an interesting record. It was obviously our first double album. We had to fight the record company about that. Record companies don't like double albums (*laughs*). We had to fight on that front and there were technical difficulties, but we overcame them.

The lead-off single from *Exile* was Tumbling Dice, which has got a great groove. You still play it live and it remains one of many people's favourite Stones tracks.

I love to play that one on stage. It's not so much the song . . . It's just a great thing to play.

Sometimes you come up with something and you think, "I could play this all night, all year." It's one of those. A lovely riff. It's got such a nice groove and a flow on it.

Are tracks such as Happy and Soul Survivor the ones where you get a real flavour of what was going on at Nellcôte?

Exactly. As I said, I can actually smell it. Because that basement hadn't been used for years. I don't think we really bothered to clean it up much. We just kind of moved in.

Happy is the quintessential *Exile* track and one of your signature songs.
Yes. To me, it was one of the benefits of actually living on top of the whole scene. Happy epitomized that. One afternoon, Jimmy Miller (producer) and Bobby Keys were there, but that was about it. The guys don't usually start work until after dark and I said: 'Look, I've got this idea. Can we just lay it down for later?' Jimmy was on drums and Bobby on baritone sax. By the time the rest of the band arrived, I'd done a few overdubs and we had finished the track. It was one of the benefits of living on top of the factory.

Was it a given that you would sing Happy? Over the years you seem to get a great kick out of doing that one live.
I think so. I'd 'stolen it' and captured it before anybody else knew it existed. So that was it. I play Happy quite a lot, more often than any of the others. I love playing it. It's not usually my genre. I'm not known for happy and joyful stuff. I'm probably more aligned to Lucifer and the dark side (*laughs*). But it was a damn good afternoon and I still love it.

Another track I love is Soul Survivor, which features loads of guitar tracks. And you've unearthed an alternate take for this release.
Yeah, that's a murky track (*laughs*). I'd have to really go back and count. There were endless overdubs. We would use a little bit from one. There's probably at least six guitars on there, in little pieces, not all the way through. But from the middle eight to the end, there's probably little bits of six overdubs going on, in and out.

Was some of the magic in the basement at Nellcôte the fact that you could tilt the amps and the sound would change as it would bounce off the walls?
Working at Nellcôte was strange because you never quite knew what you were capturing on the mobile. So inevitably, you'd do a few takes, and

then everybody would stamp up the stairs, get in the truck and have a listen. Sometimes, you had to do a bit of adjustment. It was a very interesting process. I realised slowly, as we were doing it, that this was a pretty unique way of making a record. There was something about the rhythm section sound down there—maybe it's the concrete, or maybe it's the dirt, but it had a certain sound that you couldn't replicate if you tried. Believe me, lots of people have tried.

Did you make friends with the locals while you were at Nellcôte?
Yes, a little, although we were very busy. We had a few local guys working with us. There was a chef who blew the kitchen up. There was a great explosion. Big Jacques I think his name was.

There was a lady caretaker as well, wasn't there?
She was great. How she put up with us all. . . The smile on her face all the time. I don't quite know what she was smiling at but she handled us all very correctly. I have fond memories of playing and working there. I mean there could be worse places to make a record.

There were stories that you stole power from the SNCF, the French railways. Can you admit to that after all these years?
I think we did, once or twice. Actually, it wasn't us that knew how to do it. It was a couple of local Villefrance boys (*laughs*). Yes, they did hook us to the railway line for a couple of nights when the power went.

You attracted the attention of the local police.
We had the usual amount of attention. You stand outside the front gate with the sergeant and the corporal. "Monsieur, excusez-moi." Usually things would settle down and you'd say: "Come in, have a cognac." It was like that. I can't quite remember going back that far. They were very reasonable, in their Mediterranean way. There were no big problems. Sometimes, they just wanted to come and have a look around. We did have a robbery and we got some of the guitars back. Justice prevailed. We'll leave it at that.

I know you're very fond of *Exile: The Making of Exile on Main St*, the coffee table book of the photographs Dominique Tarlé took at Nellcôte, and that you have given copies of it to friends and family. When you look at the book, does it prompt more memories?

Ah, Dominique, great guy, great photographer. We liked Dominique because he was about the most invisible photographer. You never knew he was there, he sort of melted in and became part of the band in a way. It's not often you really like to have pictures taken when you're working, but Dominique had a beautiful technique and I love the man. I was amazed by the book. I didn't know he'd taken that many pictures. A lot of people that you didn't intend to be there, like Gram Parsons for instance, ended up at Nellcôte, and stayed for a month.

There were some nice country touches on Exile. Was that because Gram had been staying with you?

We were swapping ideas. Gram taught me a lot of songs. We used to spend days singing George Jones and Merle Haggard, all the Everly Brothers harmonies. He is on *Exile* in spirit. The good die young.

You were also starting to explore a more gospel flavoured, soulful direction, something you continued doing throughout the 70s and beyond.

Yeah. Strangely enough, once we were down there, in the middle of France, we started to dig deep into American music. After all, basically, that's what we do. But we started to pull on different aspects of it, country music for instance, gospel. Maybe, because we weren't in America, we missed it. Quite honestly, down in the basement at Nellcôte, it felt like America. Especially with Bobby Keys around. It was a great room to work It was ugly, dark and damp, everything was like that . . . But, at the same time, I still have a great feeling for that basement down there. It was funky. I'll give you that (*laughs*).

Do you think, as a consequence of the fact that you were 'exiled,' that you weren't in England any more, that you thought about music differently?

Exactly. They'd kicked us out of England. That's why the album ended up being called *Exile*. We were very aware that we were suddenly out there, with our backs to the wall. We had to reinvent how to do things, make it up as we went along. In other words, there was no script, nobody had done it before. It was just a matter of necessity becoming the mother of invention.

***Exile* was started in England, at Olympic Studios in London, and at Stargroves. Then you continued in France. Why did you end up finishing the album at Sunset Sound in Los Angeles?**

In order to mix it and to do certain overdubs and other stuff we wanted. We needed rather more sophisticated equipment than what we had in our truck. That was the reason we took it there: to polish it, give it a little touch of Hollywood.

Of course, in Los Angeles, you could call on people like Billy Preston and other musicians like Dr John and various backing singers.

Bill Plummer on upright bass on a couple tracks . . . The great thing about LA, especially in those days, you could make a phone call at three in the morning and say: 'We need a couple of voices.' Within half an hour, there'd be a couple of chicks ready to go, still wearing their nightdresses (*laughs*). It was like that. You'd have an idea and it would actually happen, which was kind of cool.

Was the idea to release a double album because you were finally free from the clutches of Allen Klein, who had been your manager after Andrew Loog Oldham?

Well, there was a feeling in the air that we'd reached a schism. We'd reached breaking point with certain things that we'd done before and with certain people, Allen Klein included. So we were kind of reinventing the Stones as we went along. It was a *miracle* it happened, quite honestly. The Stones had this streak of, what do you want to call it, luck, *bonne chance*.

***Exile* is now considered a masterpiece. It's many people's favourite Stones album, but it wasn't very well received at the time.**

Maybe because it was a double album. We knew that there was going to be a sort of reaction to it in a way, just because it was very different. There were no hit singles. It was an album by itself. It shows our determination, the Stones point of view, that we insisted it was a double record, that you couldn't split it up in other words. That was what we did. We're the exiles and this is what we're doing. It was made with that kind of attitude.

The American tour that followed the release of *Exile* in 1972 was quite an eventful one. People tried to gatecrash the concerts, there were riots, you went on stage incredibly late in Boston . . .
Yeah, we've been late several times, Knebworth 1976 springs to mind. I've always been amazed at how patient some audiences have been for us. Usually, we're trying to get there. These days, obviously, we don't . . . show time is show time. But in the early days, the show started when the show started.

Because of what had happened in 1969, did you have increased security on the '72 tour? Was it different in that respect?
Well, a lot of things became different, especially about playing live around '69. I mean let alone Altamont . . . *Vive la différence* . . . Electronics and technology were starting to catch up. Suddenly, you could play with monitor speakers, you could actually hear yourself. Before that, quite honestly, you just went up there and hoped the wind was blowing the right way. Because, otherwise, you never knew what sounds were coming out or going to the audience. There was a whole lot of things going on, late 60s, early 70s. Things were changing a lot, and shows were getting bigger. Suddenly, there's football stadiums, enormous acres of people and stuff. You had to *learn* how to play these places.

Why do you think you succeeded in making that change and becoming the biggest rock'n'roll band in the world the early 70s? Do you feel there was a magic in the music that could translate to bigger crowds?
In a way, we were growing up along with the audience. If it was new to us, it was probably new to them, but it was a learning process. Quite honestly, I prefer to play in a nice little auditorium or theatre, ideally. But what are you going to do with the other 50,000 people who want to see you? So in

that respect, you just have to learn to go where the audience is and figure out how to play to them. You never know what's going to happen, that's one of the interesting things about the job—the excitement.

Over the years, you've often gone back to *Exile*. Many of the tracks work well in a live situation, like Shine a Light, which became the title of the Martin Scorsese film.
And Let It Loose and Loving Cup. We've found another take of Loving Cup for this . . . We do Rip This Joint quite often. That's one of the fastest songs in the world. That really keeps you on your toes. *Exile* is one of those records you can look at and say: 'Let's do something different.' Or Sweet Virginia, we've also done that live many, many times. And Sweet Black Angel. When you're in a little bit of doubt about what to play, or you want to play something different, basically you say: "Let's listen to *Exile* and we'll find something."

How did you decide what to add to this expanded version of *Exile*? Was it a difficult process? What did you do to the tapes? Did you go back and re-record anything?
There was talk of three, then four or five extra tracks. I'm not quite sure how we decided how many. We listened to them and we realised there were takes of Loving Cup, Soul Survivor and Tumbling Dice that would make interesting additions. And also songs that we really wanted on Exile when it was being made but we just didn't have any room for, otherwise it would have been a triple-album set. We had to draw the line somewhere and we decided that if we were going to repackage this thing and put *Exile* back out as a box set, then we should add some of the other stuff that we still had left over.

So there it is. It's kind of interesting. The tracks we found in the vaults are mostly as we left them 39 years ago. I didn't want to get in the way of what was there. I stroked an acoustic guitar here and there. Mick did new vocals for Plundered My Soul and Following the River.

Was it fun to listen back to all the out-takes and alternate takes?
Yeah, it was. Listening critically, I can hear stuff and go 'Oh my God, did

I actually play that?' Sometimes you just take off. And there's some real
. . . But, at the same time, the spirit of it and the feel of it, it's well worth
putting it out because it's the flavour of the era.

**Does the legend of *Exile*, the parties, the drugs, overshadow the reality
of what went on during those months at Nellcôte?**
We were making a record, we didn't have time! (*laughs*). Living on top
of the factory had its advantages. You went upstairs for a breath of fresh
air and a drink or two. Of course there were drugs, but it didn't affect the
work. We were out on a limb and it all came together.

**Some people were expecting live tracks from the 1972 tour as part
of the extras. There has always been talk of this great missing live
album in the Stones canon of live albums. The '72 tour is not officially
documented.**
No there's nothing live on there (*Exile* remastered). You might be right. I
might look into that. I know they put out *Get Yer Ya-Ya's Out* again. The
boxes, the all-important boxes (*laughs*).

**You had Stevie Wonder as support on the 1972 tour. You've often had
great support acts. Also The Meters in 1976.**
Ike & Tina Turner, and BB King in 1969. It was the days when shows
weren't just about one act. You had several other great bands warming up
and rocking. I kind of miss that format but *c'est la vie* . . . (*laughs*). I learnt
so much, in the early days, from playing and listening to bands that were
going on before us. Ike and Tina's band were so cool. As musicians, we'd
be checking these cats out every night and they'd be so tight. The way Ike
ran a band was phenomenal, unique.

You took a few tips from Ike?
Yeah, like that pistol-whipping piano players stuff (*laughs*).

**You've done some of your best work in France. *Exile* at Nellcôte. You've
recorded at the Pathé-Marconi studios in Paris as well, and obviously
A Bigger Bang was done at Mick's place in the Loire valley. Why do you
think it works for you in France?**

I don't know. It's strange, isn't it? Just thinking about it, I've only just realised that we've recorded in France at least as much as we have in America or England or anywhere else. Very good studios. The old Pathé-Marconi was great. It's a room you could get to know. You knew where everything was, where to put the drums. There's just something about Paris. If you've got to be somewhere for six months recording, there's nothing like a great restaurant around the corner, and a couple of crazy Frenchmen as friends.

After *Exile*, you went to Jamaica for *Goats Head Soup*. You must have liked recording in different places to get a different vibe.
We'd never recorded in Jamaica before. A lot of stuff on *Goats Head Soup* is obviously related to *Exile*. When you make records, these things sort of fold over . . . There's stuff from *Sticky Fingers* that went into *Exile* at one end and out of the other into *Goats Head Soup*. Nobody writes an album from track one to track twelve and says: 'that's it.' It's a continual process and hopefully it will continue.

I was wondering how your autobiography is coming along.
Oh! It's just about finished. I'm waiting for some proofs to come back and stuff. It's kind of weird reading about yourself, about your own life. Who'd be interested in that? (*laughs*). But then I realise there is a lot of interest so . . . It seems to be alright. I think there's some editing to do, but it's coming along. It should be out later this year.

Were there big gaps in your memory, or were you surprised how much you remembered?
I was, as much as to what I could remember, but also interviewing and talking to some of the people that were there and their version of events and trying to correlate it all. It was all very interesting, a kind of kaleidoscopic bunch of experiences. I'm hoping it will work out alright.

What memories do you have of your time in Switzerland in the 70s, after you left France?
Oh, Switzerland! First off, Switzerland was about the only country that would accept me at the time, so I'm always very grateful to the Swiss for that. Montreux, immediately, you have to mention Claude Nobs. He was

SPRINGSTEEN ON SPRINGSTEEN
Edited by Jeff Burger

Bruce Springsteen has always taken interviews seriously. As he told critic Neil Strauss in 1995, "If I have some work that I've done and want to talk about it, that's why I end up doing interviews".

Here is an unprecedented collection of Springsteen on Springsteen, spanning the past four decades.

It begins in 1973, when he is earning $75 a week and struggling to emerge from the New Jersey bar circuit.

It ends in 2012, by which time The Boss has achieved worldwide fame and has shared a platform with the likes of John Kerry and Barack Obama.

This collection features interviews by well-known media figures including US talk show host Charlie Rose, novelist Nick Hornby, and rock critics Paul Williams and Neil Strauss. It also includes rare gems from smaller periodicals that even serious Springsteen fans may not know. In addition are transcripts of radio and TV interviews that have not previously appeared in print.

Jeff Burger has covered popular music for American and international magazines and newspapers for four decades and was one of the first journalists to talk with Bruce Springsteen for a national publication. He has also published interviews with such musicians as Tom Waits, Billy Joel, the Righteous Brothers, and the members of Steely Dan. A former consulting editor at Time Inc., he has been editor of several magazines.

ISBN: 978.1.78305.041.3

Order No: OP55308

KEITH RICHARDS
THE UNAUTHORISED BIOGRAPHY
Victor Bockris

"Richards & Bockris are definitely as good as it gets"
Julie Burchill, The Spectator

If Mick Jagger is the public face of The Rolling Stones, Keith Richards has always been the band's heart, soul and musical powerhouse.

In 1992, Victor Bockris' celebrated biography was the first to recognise Richards' pivotal role in the Stones legend. Now, for the 50th anniversary of the Rolling Stones and Richards 70th birthday, the book has been fully updated by the author, incorporating the perspective of two more decades in this epic story of rock's most incredible survivor.

Here are the true facts behind:

- Richards' battles with his demons: the women, the drugs and the love-hate relationship with Jagger
- his struggle with heroin and his status as the rock star most likely to die in the 1970s
- his scarcely believable rebirth as a family man in the 1980s
- how Keith's brutally honest autobiography, *Life*, proved that behind the rebel exterior was a literate, thoughtful man of considerable intelligence, and an accomplished scholar of the blues

It is a story of pain and excess with a multiple star cast list featuring everyone from Marlon Brando and Tom Waits to Gram Parsons and Chuck Berry. It traces Richards' life from his poverty stricken roots in post-war England to his ultimate triumph on the many Stones world tours.

Bockris' unuauthorised book is illuminated with revealing quotes and thoughtful insights into the man behind the band that goes on forever. It also celebrates the one constant in Keith Richards' heroically shambolic life: his total and unwavering love of the music.

Victor Bockris, poet, interviewer and non-fiction prose writer, has spent 32 years writing about the cultural heroes of the 20th century. He is the author of major biographies of Patti Smith, John Cale, Lou Reed and many others.

ISBN: 978.1.78038.158.9
Order No: OP54318